LUCIEN GOLDMANN

CULTURAL CREATION
IN MODERN SOCIETY

INTRODUCTION BY WILLIAM MAYRL

Translated by Bart Grahl

Bibliography and Appendices compiled
by Ileana Rodriguez and Marc Zimmerman

BASIL BLACKWELL · OXFORD

Originally published as *La Création Culturelle dans la société moderne* (1971), by Les Editions Denoël, Paris, France.

Translation copyright © 1976 by Telos Press Ltd., St. Louis, Missouri.

First published in Great Britain 1977 by Basil Blackwell & Mott Ltd.

British Library Cataloguing and Publication Data

Goldmann, Lucien
  Cultural creation in modern society.
  I. Title II. Grahl, Bart
  301.2'08   CB78

  ISBN 0-631-18220-9

Printed in Great Britain by Billing & Sons Limited, Guildford, London and Worcester.

Table of Contents

Introduction, by William Mayrl   3

CULTURAL CREATION IN MODERN SOCIETY

1. The Importance of the Concept of Potential   31
   Consciousness for Communication

2. Possibilities of Cultural Action   40
   Through the Mass Media

3. The Revolt of Arts and Letters   51
   in Advanced Civilizations

4. Interdependencies between Industrial Society   76
   and New Forms of Literary Creation

5. Dialectical Thought and Transindividual Subject   89

6. The Dialectic Today   108

APPENDICES

1. A Brief Tribute to Goldmann, by Jean Piaget   123

2. Some General Comments on Lucien Goldmann,   126
   by Herbert Marcuse

3. Goldmann and Adorno: To Describe,   129
   Understand and Explain

Bibliography, compiled by Ileana Rodriguez   146
   and Marc Zimmerman

INTRODUCTION

These six essays offer the English-speaking reader an excellent overview of the thinking of one of modern France's most creative and productive social theorists.[1] They include not only some of Goldmann's last writings on mass media and mass culture, new forms of literary creativity, and avant-garde theatre and cinema, but also some of his last thoughts on the problems of social change and political organization in advanced capitalist society. Moreover, taken together, these essays provide one of the most coherent statements of Goldmann's unique methodology for a sociology of culture.

Lucien Goldmann was born in Bucharest, Romania on June 20, 1913. His early training at the University of Bucharest was in law. At the age of twenty he went to Vienna for what was to be an extremely important year of study. In addition to work in philosophy under the tutelage of the Austrian Marxist Max Adler, Goldmann encountered in Vienna the early writings of Georg Lukács. The latter experience turned out to be doubly important for Goldmann's subsequent development. In the first place, Lukács' pre-Marxist aesthetic analyses—which Goldmann later referred to as a convergence of Kantianism and phenomenology[2]—influenced the young scholar's

---

1. Other works in English are: *The Hidden God* (London: Routledge and Kegan Paul, 1964); *The Human Sciences and Philosophy* (London: Jonathan Cape, 1969); *Immanuel Kant* (London: New Left Books, 1971); *The Philosophy of the Enlightenment* (Cambridge: MIT Press, 1973) and *Racine* (Cambridge: Rivers Press, Ltd. 1972).
2. In 1970 Goldmann wrote "Although to my knowledge Lukács never admitted

selection of the subject of his life's work. Secondly, *History and Class Consciousness* convinced Goldmann of the potential of Marxism as a methodology for the analysis of culture, as well as of economy and society.

It is difficult to overemphasize the effect of *History and Class Consciousness* on Goldmann's intellectual growth. Twenty-three years and two doctoral degrees after first reading it he still considered the book to be "not only the most important work of Marxist philosophy in general, but also the most important philosophical work of the twentieth century."[3] It is not uncommon, especially in the writings of Goldmann's Zurich period, to see Lukács compared and ranked with Kant, Hegel, and Marx. And while he altered this opinion somewhat (in his 1948 Preface to the French edition of his Kant dissertation Goldmann remarked that he had come to hesitate to raise Lukács quite to the level of the founders of critical and dialectical philosophy and social science), there can be no doubt that *History and Class Consciousness* constituted the greatest single influence on Goldmann's theoretical and methodological perspective. Even after the late 1950's, when he started to articulate his approach in Piaget's language, it was still Lukács' Hegelian-Marxism which defined the real character of his thought.

According to Goldmann, the young Lukács' contribution to dialectical social science was not his social and political analyses. In fact these turned out to be quite wrong. For Goldmann the lasting value of Lukács' early work is his elaboration of the notions of totality, identity, and especially, potential consciousness.

For Lukács, the concept of totality included both structural and historical dimensions. On the level of structure, totality involves the "all-pervasive supremacy of the whole over the parts [which] is the essence of the method which Marx took over from Hegel and brilliantly transformed into the foundation of a wholly new science."[4] This idea leads to a methodological orientation markedly different from those inspired by bourgeois thought. The latter, Lukács noted, "concerns itself with objects that arise either from the process of studying phenomena in isolation, or from the division of labour and specialization in the different disciplines."[5] As a result, bourgeois

the explicit influence of phenomenology on his early work, it seems evident that the structuralist position which dominates these first writings can be explained in part by the at least implicit, if not direct, influence of Husserlian ideas." *Marxisme et sciences humaines* (Paris: Gallimard, 1970) p. 228.

3. *Structures mentales et création culturelle* (Paris: Editions Anthropos 1970), pp. 417-418.
4. Georg Lukács, *History and Class Consciousness* (London: Merlin Press, 1971), p. 27.
5. *Ibid.*, p. 28.

science is irreparably abstract.

Goldmann embraced Lukács' thinking on the totality. Indeed, he took it as the foundation of his sociological method. However, he was careful to distinguish between the effectiveness of bourgeois thought in the physical and in the human sciences. In a 1952 polemic against Georges Gurvitch, Goldmann wrote, "The second precept of the Cartesian method—'to divide each of the difficulties. . . into as many parts as possible, and as might be required for an easier solution'—valid up to a certain point in mathematics and the physico-chemical sciences, is virtually useless in the human sciences. Here the progress of knowledge proceeds, not from the simple to the complex, but from the abstract to the concrete through a continual oscillation between the whole and its parts."[6]

The idea of an oscillation between the whole and its parts provided a means by which Goldmann felt he could unite the methodological processes of interpretation and explanation, which, of necessity, remain separated in bourgeois social science. Interpretation and explanation, he maintained, are not different intellectual procedures but rather one and the same method referred to different coordinates. Interpretation involves the description of the immanent structure of the object under study. Explanation is nothing more than the insertion of the interpreted structure into an immediately encompassing structure. Thus explanation informs us of the genesis and function of the object under study. Moreover, Goldmann suggested, it is then possible to take the englobing structure as an object of interpretive study. Thus, what was explanation becomes interpretation, and explanatory research must be related to a new structure which is even wider.[7]

Goldmann was fond of using his own analysis of the tragic vision in seventeenth century France to illustrate this methodological procedure (See Chapter V). The interpretation of Pascal's *Pensées* or Racine's tragedies, he suggested, involves an understanding of how a particular vision of the world runs through these works and ties them together. Goldmann hypothesized that this vision had its origin in extremist Jansenism. And by interpreting the structure of extremist Jansenism he was able to explain the *Pensées* and the Racinian tragedies. Further, by interpreting the situation of the *noblesse de robe* under Louis XIV, one can explain the genesis and function of extremist Jansenism. And beyond this, an interpretation of social class relationships in seventeenth century France explains the situation of the *noblesse de robe*. As research continues, the

6. *The Human Sciences and Philosophy*, pp. 85-86.
7. *Marxisme et sciences humanines*, p. 66.

investigator is able to encompass more and more of the social totality under study.

However, there is more to this notion than a simply englobement of parts. In addition to being understood in a structural context, a phenomenon must be grasped as the totality of its moments of change and development. This conception goes beyond the mere description of transformed parts. As Lukács had observed of the social totality, "[history] does not resolve itself into the evolution of *contents*, of men and situations, etc. while the *principles* of society remain eternally valid."[8] To assume the existence of immutable structural forms is to be guilty of the same abstractness found in the particularistic studies of bourgeois social science. In reality, structure is always a *process* of structuration and destructuration.[9] It follows, then, that even the theoretical models and conceptual schemes of a genuine science of the totality must constantly be open to revision. Thus, for example, in one of his last papers, "The Dialectic Today" (Chapter VI), Goldmann noted how the term "capitalism" had to be transformed from Marx's original usage to "imperialism" by Lenin and Luxemburg, and that their conception has to be modified again in order to reflect the "managed" nature of contemporary advanced capitalism.

The upshot of the historical dimension of the social totality is that the more sociology becomes a science of social forms, the less it can tell us about society. However, this should not be taken to imply that Goldmann (or Lukács) abjured all universal judgments. In a paper written in 1947 on the philosophical dimensions of dialectical materialism,[10] Goldmann noted that although this position defines man by his historical character, it does admit of a limited number of propositions which are transhistorically valid. Among judgments of fact in this category he included the unity of subject and object with regard to knowledge in general, and the partial or total identity of subject and object when it is a question of knowledge of human facts; the social and historical character of all human activity and its manifestations; the dialectical character of all individual or collective life; and so forth.[11] As for judgments of value, he noted that the humanistic and dialectical materialist accepts a number of the values developed by the progressive bourgeoisie in its struggles against feudalism. The values of "life," "liberty," and "happiness," for instance, are retained in dialectical thought and joined by a radically new value of "community." Moreover this new value is under-

8. *History and Class Consciousness*, p. 47.
9. See, *Marxisme et sciences humaines*, p. 221.
10. See, *Recherches dialectiques* (Paris: Gallimard, 1959) pp. 11-25.
11. *Ibid.*, p. 13.

stood as the historical precondition for the fulfillment of the earlier ones. The quest for human community—which, in its highest form, is the struggle for communism—is a striving for totality whether it proceeds in art and philosophy or in political action.

Goldmann's construal of these transhistorical judgments is reminiscent of the young Lukács' approach to communism. Paul Breines has rightly used the term "wager" (which Lukács had appropriated from Kierkegaard) with regard to Lukács' conversion to left Hegelianism and communism:[12] "[Lukács'] conceptions of Communist revolution as 'redemption of the world' and [his] image of Communist revolutionaries standing with clear conscience before no lesser a court of judgment than that constituted by the great poets, the class conscious proletariat and truth itself, are particularly vivid but not uncharacteristic signs of the deep spiritual continuity between the 'old' and the 'new' Lukács. Specifically, they indicate the great extent to which the initial phase of Lukács' Marxism was formed by primarily ethical and philosophical rather than political considerations."[13] I think there can be little doubt that Lukács retained strong elements of his early Kantian and existentialist positions at least well into the first decade of his Marxism. With Goldmann, whose introduction to Marxism came through the Kantian Marxist Max Adler as well as the early Lukács, these ethical-philosophical elements never diminish.[14] For instance, in 1954, a full twenty-one years after his encounters with Adler and Lukács, Goldmann maintained that Marxism was essentially a matter of faith: "Marxist faith is faith in the future which men make for themselves in and through history...It would be just as absurd for Pascal or Kant to deny the existence of God on empirical grounds as it would be for Marx to use the same criterion to assert or deny the validity of the idea of progress or of humanity's march towards socialism. In both cases the intital wager [Goldmann appropriated the term from Pascal] depends on an act of faith, on 'reasons of the heart' in Pascal, or the validity of reason in Kant and Marx, a wager which goes beyond and integrates theory and practice."[15] The fact that Goldmann never overcame the ethical-philosophical origins of his Marxism is evidenced in his work on art and society as well as in his political commentaries.

---

12. Paul Breines, *Lukács and Korsch 1910-1932: A Study of the Genesis and Impact of* Geschichte und Klassenbewusstwein *and* Marxismus und Philosophie, (University Microfilms, Inc. Ann Arbor, 1972), p. 96.

13. *Ibid.*, p. 100.

14. See Goldmann's discussion of Max Adler and the problems of values in Marxism in "Y a-t-il une sociologie marxiste?" in *Recherches dialectiques*, pp. 280-302.

15. *The Hidden God*, p. 90 and 92. See also Goldmann's discussion of Pascal's Wager, pp. 283-302.

Several authors have recently argued that the rejection of the theory of the objective crash of capitalism by many of the leading theoreticians of the Second International was linked to their essentially left-ethical and Kantian orientations.[16] For example, Russell Jacoby observes that "[t]he link between a revisionist theory that rejected a breakdown and a policy of practical piecemeal reforms is not far afield. If there were no objective collapse, the necessity for socialism shifted solely to a subjective and idealist dimension which could only move within the status quo."[17] In this light, it is more than coincidence that when in the 1960s Goldmann turned to the problems of cultural creation in modern society, he used a model of capitalist development which bore a striking resemblance to one put forth by Hilferding thirty years earlier. Indeed, he even used Hilferding's term "organizational capitalism" to characterize an economy which had survived the "terminal crisis" predicted by traditional Marxists. Moreover, consistent with this general pattern is the fact that up to his death Goldmann considered himself a "revolutionary-reformist."[18] The latter position involves abandoning the idea of a proletarian revolution and replacing it with the notion of a gradual, albeit radical, transformation of the present productive apparatus toward various forms of self-management by the collective producers. I will spend more time on Goldmann's revolutionary-reformism below when I discuss his political thinking and activity, especially with regard to the events of May 1968. At this point it is enough to note that while Goldmann rejected a good many of the social and political aspects of *History and Class Consciousness*, he held steadfast to most of its ethical and philosophical components. There is one significant exception to this, to which I will now turn.

For Hegel the identity of the subject and object of thought was total, since reality was constituted by rationality. Lukács realized the necessity of separating the "merely objective" dialectics of nature from those of society, because in the latter "the subject is included in the reciprocal relation in which theory and practice become dialectical with reference to one another."[19] However, within the human realm, Lukács maintained, the identity of subject and object is total. Goldmann followed Lukács in the separation of the realms of

---

16. See Lucio Colletti, *From Rousseau to Lenin* (London: New Left Books, 1972), especially the chapter on Bernstein and the 2nd International; and "The Theory of the Crash," *Telos* 13 (Fall, 1972); and Russell Jacoby, "The Politics of the Crisis Theory," *Telos* 23 (Spring, 1975).

17. Jacoby, *Ibid.*, p. 29.

18. See his Preface to *Marxisme et sciences humaines* which was written only days before his death in early October 1970.

19. *History and Class Consciousness*, p. 207.

nature and society. Furthermore, he fully appreciated the idea that in the human sciences knowledge itself becomes part of the social consciousness. By the late 1940's, however, probably due to the influence of his teacher and friend Jean Piaget, Goldmann was questioning the idea of a total identity in the human realm. And by the mid-1960's, under the increasingly apparent influence of Freud, he had rejected this idea altogether, retaining only the notion of a partial identity. In effect, he limited the possibility of identity to the collective or, as he called it, the transindividual subject.

The individual person, Goldmann maintained, is made up of both a libidinal and a social structure.[20] In the former, which is essentially biological and therefore legitimately within the sphere of the natural sciences, the relations between knower and known are subject-object relations. Insofar as it is the nature of certain libidinal processes to be non-conscious they cannot, by definition, become aware of themselves as subjects. Or, approached from a different angle, while these processes contribute to the constitution of the individual subject they are not constituted by that subject. The social component of the individual, on the other hand, presents an entirely different situation: here the structural processes are the creation of numerous subjects, each of which is partially constituted by the others. Put in another way, the *social* person consists of symbolic and significative structures which originate only in the social division of labor. Therefore the study of the relations which make up this division of labor is, in a very real way, an exercise in social self-consciousness. Moreover, given the historical character of the division of labor and the social totality constituted by it, even the study of events and struggles long past can generate consciousness as well as scientific knowledge. In 1952 Goldmann wrote: "If knowledge of history has any practical importance for us, it is because we learn from it about men who, in *different* circumstances and with *different* means for the most part inapplicable in our own time, fought for values and ideals which were similar, identical, or opposed to those of today; and this makes us conscious of belonging to a totality which transcends us, which we support in the present and which men who come after us will continue to support in the future."[21] The study of artistic creations can have the same function. Roy Pascal quotes Lukács as observing that "art awakens our historical self-consciousness and keeps it awake." Indeed, "the great literature of the past is meaningful to us because it

---

20. One of Goldmann's most complete discussions of the relations between libidinal and social structures is his paper "Le sujet de la création culturelle" in *Marxisme et sciences humaines*, pp. 94-120.

21. *The Human Sciences and Philosophy*, p. 29.

is mankind's living memory of its past, akin to the childhood memories of an individual man."[22]

The idea that human science, aesthetic creation, and for that matter, any products of human consciousness, can be relevant to the actual struggles of social subjects was one of Lukács' most influential contributions to Goldmann's methodological orientation. For, coupled as it later was with insights derived from Piaget's epistemological and psychological researches, it rounded out the basic methodological perspective which Goldmann hoped to apply not only to aesthetic productions but to human reality in general. The transitional link between the philosophy of identity and Piaget's genetic epistemology was provided by Lukács' notion of "ascribed" or, in Goldmann's terms, "potential" consciousness.

It is well known that Lukács began his analysis of class consciousness with Marx's distinctions between the consciousness of this or that proletarian and the consciousness of the proletarian class. Probably under the influence of Weber as much as of Hegel and Marx, Lukács defined the consciousness of a class as an objective possibility rooted in the social and historical totality. In brief, class consciousness consisted in the thoughts and feelings which members of a class would have *if they were able* to assess their objective situation correctly. Class consciousness, then, is neither the sum nor the average of what is thought by individuals. The latter would be what Lukács referred to as psychological or empirical consciousness. Class consciousness is rather "the appropriate and rational reaction 'imputed' to a particular typical position in the process of production."[23]

Goldmann considered Lukács' development of the concept of potential consciousness to be his major methodological contribution to the human sciences.[24] More than any of the other dialectical notions, it provides a concrete starting point for empirical social research (see Chapter I). However, underlying the methodological value of the concept of potential consciousness is the broader issue of the function of human consciousness in general. Goldmann felt that one of the fullest elaborations of this issue and of its implications for all human activity could be found in the work of the non-Marxist psychologist Piaget. Indeed, Goldmann often remarked that the fact that Piaget unwittingly developed the thinking of Marx and Lukács in pursuing his own interests and research, provided independent

22. Roy Pascal, "Georg Lukács: The Concept of Totality" in *Georg Lukács*, edited by G.H.R. Parkinson (New York: Random House, 1970) pp. 147-171. The quoted passage appears on p. 153.
23. *History and Class Consciousness*, p. 51.
24. *Marxisme et sciences humaines*, p. 238.

verification of dialectical materialism.[25] In any event, the encounter with Piaget and his work provided Goldmann not only with new insights into the nature of human activity but also with a new language through which to present his dialectical research.

Goldmann led an active intellectual life in the eleven years between his departure from Vienna and his arrival in Geneva to work with Piaget. In 1934 he went to Paris to continue his studies. In the next five years he obtained French degrees in law, political science and literature. (His interest in the latter area was undoubtedly related to his discovery of Lukács' first two books in Vienna.) In 1940, when the French capitulated to the Nazis, Goldmann fled to neutral Switzerland. There he resumed his studies of German philosophy, focusing on the aesthetic and ethical writings of Kant. His manuscript *Mensch, Gemeinschaft und Welt in der Philosophie Immanuel Kants* was accepted as a doctoral thesis at the University of Zurich in 1945. That same year Goldmann moved to Geneva and the position of research assistant at the Laboratoire de Psychologie de Genève. In 1948, over a year after he had returned to Paris, and again in 1952, Goldmann wrote papers on the contributions of genetic psychology and epistemology to dialectical social science.

Piaget—although he was originally unaware of the affinity—recognized with Marx that consciousness is a process involved in the interaction between human beings and their environments. All psychic facts result from a cyclical process of adaptation which Piaget described as assimilation and accommodation.[26] The subject assimilates the environment into its schemes of thought and action, and at the same time accommodates itself to the resistant environment. Goldmann observed both dynamic and conservative implications in this process. It is dynamic in that the subject attempts to extend its sphere of action to a larger and larger part of the surrounding world. It is conservative in that the subject endeavors to preserve its own internal structures of thought and activity and to impose them on the world. However, the world is not always easily assimilated, and the subject must constantly readapt itself by creating new structures of thought and action.[27] Moreover, when the world is successfully transformed, new structures of activity became necessary to assimilate the new reality. Thus, through constant interaction with its environment the subject continually transforms itself.

The reader, of course, will recognize the striking similarity between

25. See, for example, *Recherches dialectiques*, especially pp. 118-145 and *Marxisme et sciences humaines* pp. 17-30 for discussions of the relation of Piaget to Marx and Lukács.
26. *Recherches dialectiques*, p. 129.
27. *Ibid.*, p. 130.

Piaget's thinking in this regard and Marx's writings on the labor process.[28] In 1956 Goldmann was able to note that Piaget had started to quote Marx on this point. (I'm sure this was due, at least in part, to Goldmann's continuing influence on Piaget.) In any event, Piaget's idea that human beings are constantly attempting to adapt to or to transcend their environments through their thought and action introduced a new dimension into the problem of potential consciousness. For underlying the question of the maximum possible awareness of a given group is the issue of the *adequacy* of its structure of consciousness to the task of establishing or maintaining an equilibrium between the group and its environment.

In addition to his masterful explication of the dialectical relation between consciousness and activity, Piaget influenced Goldmann in several other ways. In the first place, genetic epistemology and psychology seemed to establish the efficacy of Marx's anthropology through careful and systematic empirical research. It was significant, Goldmann thought, that a respected scientist not associated with Marxism could develop and defend the notion of an historical totality in an intellectual atmosphere so dominated by logical positivism that even many Marxists had fallen prey to it. Secondly, Piaget's research extended the application of a genetic perspective into areas like mathematics, formal logic, biology and psychology. Indeed, Goldmann felt that Piaget's genetic research went far in providing a psychology which would complement historical and dialectical materialism. For the most part, previous attempts in this area had involved little more than the attachment of Watsonian behaviorism to mechanistic materialism.[29] Finally, and in retrospect perhaps most importantly, Piaget's work provided a language which enabled Goldmann to engage in a critical dialogue with structuralism, the major intellectual expression of modern organizational capitalism.[30]

---

28. See, for example, *Capital I* (Moscow: Foreign Languages Publishing House, 1961), pp. 177ff.

29. See, *Recherches dialectiques*, pp. 127-128. In this regard Goldmann had arrived at a conclusion similar to that which Soviet psychologist L.S. Vygotsky had come to several decades earlier from a different point of departure. See Vygotsky, *Thought and Language* (Cambridge: The MIT Press, 1962).

30. Of course, "Goldmann's analysis of Levi-Strauss, the early Althusser, and other formalistic structuralists owes more to Piaget than its language. Goldmann criticises the structuralists for their elimination of the dynamic subject whose action is functional with respect to the accommodation and assimilation of the ambient world (See Chapter four). He felt that while the method inspired by structural linguistics may be well suited to the analysis of the formal aspects of language, it is bound to be inadequate for the explication of cultural productions *even though the latter may be justly considered communicative acts*. In brief, the modern structural method permits, at best, the study of *la langue* and not *la parole*. In other words, it can study the *means* which permit the expression of meaning, but not the meaningful structures themselves. (See, *Structures mentales et création culturelle*, pp. 14-15.)

It is interesting to note that Goldmann did not begin to use Piaget's structuralist language until almost twelve years after he had left Geneva. Indeed, the first two major works published after his return to Paris, *Sciences humaines et philosophie* (1952) and *Le dieu caché* (1956) virtually ignore Piaget. This is especially noteworthy with regard to the latter work. Goldmann labored from 1949 to 1956 on *Le dieu caché*, his doctoral thesis for the Sorbonne. In translation the book runs to some four hundred pages, yet there are a mere six references to Piaget. And these are all remarks in passing, parenthetical comments or footnotes. However, only three years later Goldmann published *Recherches dialectiques*, a collection of essays he had written between 1945 and 1958, and dedicated them to "Jean Piaget, le maitre et l'ami." In addition to the two papers on Piaget mentioned earlier, the collection included a chapter written in 1958 on "Le concept de structure significative en histoire de la culture." This piece seems to me to mark a shift in Goldmann's language and mode of presentation. In it, for example, the concept of the "totality" or "whole" became "meaningful structure," and dialectical materialism began to be presented as a form of structuralism. Within a few years Goldmann was referring to his methodological orientation almost exclusively as "genetic structuralism." Furthermore, the works of Hegel, Marx, Lukács, and even Freud were soon "christened" with this new name.

Along with the new structuralist terminology, the period after 1959 saw several other changes in Goldmann's life and work. From 1958 he had been Directeur de'Etudes in the VI Section of the Ecole Pratique des Hautes Etudes in Paris. In 1961 he accepted the Directorship of the Centre de Recherches de Sociologie de la Litterature at the Sociological Institute of the Free University in Brussels. After that time there was a marked shift in Goldmann's substantive research. He began to turn away from those classics of the 17th, 18th, and 19th centuries which Lukács had considered great examples of literary realism to the kind of modernist, avant-garde productions which the latter had dismissed as expressions of bourgeois decadence. Although this turn represents somewhat of a break with Lukácsian aesthetics it is not as sharp as some have made it out. In the first place, Lukács himself seems to have tempered his position on modernism in the last few decades of his life.[31] Secondly, Lukács' aesthetic analyses remained the foundation of Goldmann's methodology even in its final, genetic structuralist, phase.

Shortly before his death in 1970 Goldmann wrote a brief essay on the aesthetics of the young Lukács.[32] What strikes the reader of these fourteen pages is that the points highlighted in the review of Lukács' first three books virtually exhaust his contribution to Goldmann's model for a sociology of literary creation. On the level of aesthetic analysis, as well as in the general theoretical model we have been discussing in the previous pages, for all practical purposes, Lukács' influence seemed to have stopped with his writings up to 1926. According to Goldmann, Lukács' early works should not be read in chronological order. Just as Marx noted that the key to the anatomy of the ape was the anatomy of man, so for Goldmann *History and Class Consciousness* is the key to *The Soul and the Forms* (1911) and *The Theory of the Novel* (1916).[33]

In 1970 Goldmann contended that from the vantage point of 1923, we can see a continuous evolution in Lukács, from a limited (to aesthetics) and static structuralism to a generalized, genetic structuralism. Moreover, all of the elements in this process are essential to its outcome: one cannot disregard the two early works. Indeed, Goldmann traced one of this most important concepts, the meaningful structure, to *The Soul and the Forms*. The essential idea of that work, he noted, is that "spiritual values in general and literary and philosophical values in particular are rooted in a certain number of forms, of coherent structures which permit the human soul to express its different possibilities."[34] However, as we saw, these forms are static and are limited to artistic expression. It is only in *History and Class Consciousness* that we get an image of human beings striving through their activity and thought to create wider and wider meaningful structures for the purpose of coping with and transforming their environment.[35] Thus, the forms have become historical and general. We can speak no longer of structure, but rather of structuration and destructuration. Moreover the forms are no longer the sole creations of artists but of transindividual subjects, especially of social classes. In summary, Goldmann credited Lukács' three early works with the ideas that 1) man is an historical being who attempts to give significance to his life, 2) history, human creation, is

32. *Marxisme et sciences humaines*, pp. 227-241.
33. *Ibid.*, p. 233.
34. *Ibid.*, p. 234. In his Zurich thesis Goldmann tied the aesthetics of the young Lukács to Kant's aesthetics. He noted that the two basic components of Kant's "judgments of taste" were 1) In the aesthetic field, empirical man can overcome his limitations and attain the totality, and 2) Aesthetic judgments do not relate to the reality of objects or events but only their *form*. See, *Immanuel Kant*, pp. 182ff.
35. Silvia Federici traces this evolution beyond *History and Class Consciousness* to Lukács' later aesthetics. See her "Notes on Lukács' Aesthetics," *Telos* 11, (Spring, 1972) pp. 141-151.

thus meaningful and admits the validity of the category of progress, and 3) spiritual (or cultural) creations are special forms of activity which have as one of their principal goals the establishment of consistency and coherence.[36]

Between 1964 and 1967 Goldmann published several systematic statements of the genetic structuralist approach to literary creation.[37] In them the influence of the young Lukács is extremely evident. In the first place, the three fundamental characteristics of human behavior which are "basic to all positive research into literary creation"[38] are none other than the three ideas he later credited to the early Lukács. Beyond this, however, even the operational premises of genetic structuralism are extensively indebted to Lukács, especially to *The Soul and the Forms.*

The first working premise of Goldmann's model for the analysis of cultural creation is that the essential relation between social life and literary creation does not involve the content of these two spheres but instead what he called "the form of the content."[39] This form refers to the mental structures which organize the empirical consciousness of a particular group as well as the imaginary universe created by the writer.[40] A second closely related premise is that the researcher will often be able to discover a more or less rigorous homology between the mental structures of a certain group and the imaginary universe created by the writer. The quest for homologous structures, Goldmann warned, often involves a great deal of painstaking research. Frequently, entirely different contents reveal themselves to be structurally homologous once the investigator finds the functional link between them.[41] For example, Goldmann observed of the relations between Racine's tragedies and the vision of the world of radical Jansenism, i.e. its meaningful structure, that ". . . it is not the Christian dramas like *Esther* and *Athalie*, but the pagan plays like *Andromaque, Britannicus* and *Phèdre* which prove to be most closely linked to [Jansenist] theology." For it is these latter plays which, in spite of their manifest content, most clearly evidence a "hidden god who demands absolute obedience to contradictory obligations, and

36. *Marxisme et sciences humaines*, p. 234.
37. See, for example, *Pour une sociologie du roman* (Paris: Gallimard, 1964) pp. 337-372; *Marxisme et sciences humaines* pp. 54-93; "Structure: Reality and Concept" in R. Macksey and E. Donato (eds.) *The Structuralist Controversy* (Baltimore: The Johns Hopkins Press, 1972) pp. 98-124; and " 'Genetic Structuralism' in the Sociology of Literature" in Elizabeth and Tom Burns (eds.) *Sociology of Literature and Drama* (Penguin Books. 1973) pp. 109-123.
38. " 'Genetic Structuralism' in the Sociology of Literature," p. 118.
39. "Structure: Reality and Concept," p. 106.
40. *Marxisme et sciences humaines*, p. 57.
41. *Ibid.*, p. 58.

who is manifest, each time that man must act in the world, through precisely this contradiction."[42]

Just as the notion of the form of the content can be traced to Lukács' first German publications, so too the idea of homologous structures found its major inspiration in the young Lukács. Goldmann maintained that in the "phenomenological" writings of Lukács from as early as 1908 one can detect the glimmer of a realization that economic forms based on production for exchange rather than for use tend to duplicate themselves structurally in social consciousness.[43] However, it wasn't for another decade, after encounters with Georg Simmel and Max Weber and especially after his reconsideration of Marx, that Lukács was able to develop his theory of reification (see chapters II and III for Goldmann's discussion and use of the theory of reification). Using *History and Class Consciousness* as a key to the earlier works, Goldmann re-examined *The Theory of the Novel* and came up with a hypothesis which helped guide his last decade of work. There exists, he suggested, "a *rigorous homology* between the literary form of the novel...and the everyday relation of men with goods in general and, by extension, of men with each other, in a society which produces for the market."[44] The reader will recognize the impact of this hypothesis in Chapters II, III and IV. What is important to point out in the present context is that the quest for structural homologies, especially in Goldmann's later works, is dominated by the theme of reification and the possibilities of overcoming it.

A third, and extremely important, premise of genetic structuralist cultural analysis is that the individual artist does not create world visions. He or she expresses the collective mental productions of a group. In this sense artistic work represents an intersection of individual and collective consciousness. Only the group can develop the categories that structure its activities. However, it is the artist, the philosopher, and even the scientist who, on their respective conceptual planes, express these categories at a high level of consistency and coherence.[45] Two additional premises flow from this. In the first place, genetic structuralism eschews analyses of literary creations in terms either of the psycho-biography of authors, or of purely immanent, i.e., "phenomenological," analysis of the works' meaning structures, or of the work as a simple reflection of collective

---

42. " 'Genetic Structuralism' in the Sociology of Literature," p. 121.

43. *Marxisme et sciences humaines*, p. 236.

44. *Pour une sociologie du roman*, p. 36. A translation of the First Chapter of this work appears in *Telos* 18 (Winter, 1974) 122-135.

45. *Marxisme et sciences humaines*, pp. 57-58. Also Chapter IV of the present volume.

consciousness. Goldmann admits that each of these three approaches can uncover valuable information concerning a writer, his or her work, and society. However, from the perspective of the totality they are all sorely lacking. For example, the psychoanalyst might tell us that Racine wrote his tragedies in order to relieve libidinal tension. [46] And it is quite possible this is true. However, it tells us nothing about the meaningful structure expressed by those plays. For that, one must go beyond Racine's psyche to a transindividual subject whose mental structures correspond to the form of the content of the tragedies. Or, again, there have undoubtedly been thousands of brother-sister relationships exactly like the particular relationship between Blaise Pascal and his sister Jacqueline. However, it was only at a certain moment, in a certain historical context, that this relationship exerted a favorable influence on the expression of a philosophical system which embodied a world vision elaborated by radical Jansenists at Port-Royal. [47] It is this latter aspect we must understand, and not the relations between Blaise and Jacqueline, if we want to grasp the significance of the *Pensées*. Phenomenology presents a similar problem. While an immanent analysis of a work without recourse to facts "external" to it can be useful and, in rare cases, depending upon the genius of the investigator, [48] can uncover the meaningful structure of the work in question, reliance on this method tends to obscure rather than to clarify. Interpretation must be supplemented with explanation. In order to achieve a full understanding of a cultural product, the researcher has to englobe its internal structure by wider and wider structures. It is in these latter structures that the internal meaning of a work has its genesis and function.

The method which tries to understand a work as a simple reflection of the content of collective consciousness, i.e., traditional empirical sociology, has a different kind of problem than do the psychoanalytic and phenomenological approaches. Practicioners of this method realize that the explanation of a work must go beyond the individual author and even beyond the work itself, to the collective consciousness which it reflects. However, by focusing on the *content* of collective consciousness, traditional sociology ignores the most important function of aesthetic production. Art does on the plane of the imaginary what philosophy does on the level of the rational concept. Along with philosophy, and sometimes science, aesthetic creations,

---

46. See, *Ibid.*, pp. 94-120.
47. *Ibid.*, pp. 112-113.
48. Goldmann used the young Lukács and certain periods in the life of Sartre to illustrate this rare phenomenological genius. *Structures mentales et création culturelle*, pp. 11-12.

especially literature, help to clarify and make coherent the strivings of social subjects to achieve or maintain dynamic equilibrum with their environments. An interesting consequence of the traditional empirical approach to aesthetic work, is its inability to deal with outstanding and obviously creative artistic productions. Empirical sociology, Goldmann often remarked, has extraordinary success with mediocre art.[49] This is because while every artist puts into his or her work something of what he or she has experienced and lived through, the more mediocre artists are confined to those experiences. They invent little . nd are therefore likely to produce simple reflections of their ambient world. In brief, they express the real rather than the potential consciousness of the group or society to which they belong. Therefore a fifth working premise of genetic structural literary analysis is that it seeks out summits of literature, theatre and cultural creation in general.[50] This latter premise has earned for Goldmann a criticism similar to that leveled against Lukács: both have been accused of being elitist, even aristocratic, in their taste for the classics of enlightenment and bourgeois art. That Goldmann was willing to consider recent works like those of Malraux, Robbe-Grillet and Genet does not change matters in this regard. Although the value of these authors within the genetic structuralist perspective lies in their ability to express the possibilities of contemporary industrial society, critics continue to claim that in the final analysis Goldmann considered the productions of these writers to be a significant cut above the works of ordinary mortals.

Goldmann's selection of art is not the only thing that earned him the label of elitism. His politics have also occasionally given rise to that approbation. I would like to conclude with a brief look at Goldmann's political theory and practice, since it provides an important context for understanding especially the last decade of his work.

Goldmann's politics are important both in terms of their content and the form of that content. Indeed, with regard to the latter, one is tempted to suggest that there is a "rigorous structural homology" between Goldmann's approaches to methodology and aesthetic analysis, and his political writings and activity. Genetic structuralism might be viewed as an attempt to introduce dialectical materialism into modern intellectual life by, as it were, boring from within. Revolutionary-reformism seems to have the same function for socialism.

---

49. See *Marxisme et sciences humaines*, p. 57 and "Structure: Reality and Concept," p. 107 for a discussion of sociological analysis and mediocre art.
50. *Marxisme et sciences humaines*, p. 58.

The substance of Goldmann's political thinking is closely related to his analysis of cultural creation in contemporary industrial society. Since that analysis constitutes the major topic of this book, I will trace its broad contours only far enough to show its relation to his politics. It was noted earlier that the historical dimension of the social totality implies that even the categories and conceptual schemes of a genuinely dialectical science must be constantly revised to cope with an ever changing social reality. Goldmann felt that this principle simply amounted to the application of a Marxist approach to Marxist studies.

According to Goldmann, many important aspects of the original efforts of Marx and Engels and their immediate successors retain their full value today. This is especially so with respect to their basic dialectical orientation and their materialist conception of human history. However, it is also true with respect to much of their concrete research. Indeed, Goldmann felt that the analyses of commodity fetishism—especially when they are seen through the lens provided by Lukács' theory of reification—were more relevant to contemporary society than they were to the reality of Marx's day.

On the other hand, there have been developments which Marx and his most brilliant followers—not to mention his epigones—could not foresee, even though the Marxist method makes them perfectly understandable in retrospect. The most important of these include, first, the ability of capitalist economies to be "managed" and even "fine-tuned" so as to obviate the formerly constant danger of crisis, and secondly, the absence in contemporary Western society of the predicted increasing pauperization of the working class. As a result of these historical developments (and non-developments), Goldmann felt that a large part of Marx's theory of the revolutionary potential of the working class had to be revised. Certainly the working class was not destined to be the identical subject-object of history, as both the young Marx and the young Lukács had thought. (As we saw earlier, Goldmann's adherence to Piaget and his limited adherence to Freud, among other influences, had given him theoretical and methodological grounds for rejecting Lukács' notion of total identity.) The upshot of this changed reality is that analyses of contemporary society in terms of many of the concepts and struggles of the late 19th and early 20th centuries are dogmatic, theoretically rigid, and unimaginative.[51] Moreover, they are bound to result in error and, worse, in political miscalculation.

In contrast, Goldmann felt that the studies of Adorno,

---

51. *Ibid.*, pp. 312ff.

Horkheimer, Marcuse, and Habermas were much closer to modern reality. For the research of the Frankfurt School theorists started with the recognition of the "managed" character of modern capitalist society, the penetrating effects of reification on consciousness and daily life, and the changed character and function of the traditional working class. In this perspective, Western capitalism since World War II has been characterized by an increasing stability in the economic sector brought about by state intervention on behalf of the large monopolies. Along with a rationalization of market processes has come a rationalization in all spheres of social and cultural life. In the process, the last remnants of individual autonomy and creativity, which were the byproducts of the free market of liberal capitalism, are being smothered in a mode of production and administration which requires greater levels of consumption, greater state intervention, and highly trained and specialized, but basically passive, technicians and bureaucrats. The major part of the population, although experiencing a higher standard of living, have been reduced to a status of administered passivity as consumers of mass education, mass media, and mass leisure. For the first time since the feudal epoch there exists a growing sense of totality within the collective consciousness. Yet far from reflecting the unity of a human community, the current totalization of society is rooted in the need for modern capitalism to organize and rationalize production and consumption on a global level. Thus the world vision expressed by the most significant philosophies of this period reflect an obsession with the organization of the whole. In spite of their differences, modern functionalism and structuralism along with the various "systems" theories are thoroughly holistic. Gone is the focus on the individual part found in the rationalism and empiricism of earlier liberal capitalism. The empahsis is now on the *interrelation* of system parts rather than the parts themselves. This change has been especially apparent in the human sciences, where structuralism has implied a totality which, for all practical purposes, is devoid of human beings and history.

Not only was Goldmann in general agreement with the foregoing analysis of modern capitalist society, he contributed substantially to it in the writings of his last decade. However, there was one significant point on which he felt that the theorists of the technological totality were as lacking in theoretical imagination as the dogmatists of the Third International.[52] For Goldmann, the conclusion that the rationalized economy and culture of contemporary society, along with

---

52. *Ibid.*, p. 315.

its rising standards of living, had eliminated all sources of critical thought and action merely confounded the real and the possible. While it was true that the traditional working class was shrinking in size, influence, and critical consciousness, Goldmann felt that other strata were emerging which had the potential to turn modern society away from the path of technological and bureaucratic totalitarianism toward socialist humanism. Consequently, at this point he turned away from the pessimistic writings of the Frankfurt School, especially those of Marcuse, to the analyses of the Italian theorists Victor Foa and Bruno Tretin and their French followers Serge Mallet and André Gorz.

Goldmann didn't like the concept "new working class." He felt it made potentially confusing concessions to the traditional analysis. [53] However, on the basis of his own investigations of contemporary and avant-garde art forms, as well as by the writings of the Italian and French proponents of the term, he was convinced that the analyses which generated this concept were essentially correct.

The "salaried middle levels," as Goldmann described them—the highly educated and specialized technicians, bureaucrats, teachers, social service workers, etc.—constitute a stratum which to an increasing degree is replacing the traditional working class in economic and social importance. Moreover, this stratum is starting to take on the functions of an earlier group which Goldmann referred to as "notables": i.e., the old middle class of independent gentlemen which had been the source of a large number of intellectuals attached both to the bourgeoisie, as advisors, accountants, etc., and to the working class movements as theorists and organizers. In terms of their potential for developing critical consciousness, the members of this new stratum are at a disadvantage *vis-à-vis* the earlier notables due to their relative lack of independence. Intellectuals are more and more being attached to and dependent upon large scale private and governmental organizations. But members of this stratum have a double advantage over the traditional working class. Because of their skills and education the members of the new middle stratum are indispensable to the economy. Therefore, they enjoy a high degree of job security. Furthermore, the salaries of the new middle level workers are increasing and, Goldmann thought, will doubtless continue to do so. [54] These three factors taken together would seem to confirm the pessimistic analyses of the Frankfurt School. Lack of independence,

---

53. *Ibid.*, p. 277.
54. "Reflections on *History and Class Consciousness*" in István Mészaros (ed.) *Aspects of History and Class Consciousness* (London: Routledge and Kegan Paul, 1971) pp. 65-84.

along with a high level of job security, and ever increasing standards of living, would provide the ideal backdrop for the emergence of what C. Wright Mills called "the cheerful robot." However, Goldmann and the theorists of the new working class saw another side to this picture, a growing contradiction. As you continue to increase a group's economic rewards, the law of diminishing returns starts to set in: economic rewards come to have less value. If this process continues workers will start to concern themselves with the organization of their workplaces.[55] Therein lies the radical potential of the new salaried middle stratum. But are there in fact any indications that this potential is being brought to fruition? In the early 1960's, long before the revolt of students and intellectuals in most Western societies, Goldmann felt his cultural analyses were leading to an affirmative answer.

Earlier we saw that for the genetic structuralist, genuine art has the function of pushing the collective categories to their maximum level of consistency and coherence. Consequently, art can tell at least as much about society as an understanding of social structure can tell about art. In the course of his studies of the novels of Robbe-Grillet[56] and the theatre of Jean Genet,[57] Goldmann came to the conclusion that although the potential for critical consciousness does exist in modern society, it is beset by several problems. In the first place, in a society in which the value of the individual has disappeared from both the marketplace and collective consciousness, it is no longer possible to present the real problems confronting people in society by means of easily perceived, concrete stories. According to Goldmann, "the biography of a character has become merely anecdotal." "Narration restricted to things and events at the immediately lived level risks remaining in miscellaneous fact with no essential meaning" (see Chapter III). By the same token, if a writer tries to express the reality of contemporary society, he or she must move to such a level of abstraction as to risk misunderstanding by the general public. Thus, for example, when in *La Jalousie*, Robbe-Grillet writes "The light, rubber-soled shoes make no sound on the hallway tiles," it is usually interpreted on a mundane, immediately perceived level. The jealous husband walks softly to surprise his wife. However, this overlooks Robbe-Grillet's actual mode of expression. In his works, innate objects dominate over human activities. Indeed, things become the

55. *Ibid.*, p. 80.
56. See *Pour une sociologie du roman*, pp. 277-334 and *Structures mentales et création culturelle*, pp. 167-192, as well as Chapters III and IV of the present volume.
57. In addition to Chapter III of this book, see *Structures mentales et création culturelle*, pp. 267-325.

sole reality. Jealousy, for example, is indicated not by human activity but rather by the presence of a third chair, a third glass, etc. The husband does not walk softly, instead, the rubber-soled shoes make no sound.[58] Yet, in spite of frequent misinterpretation, Robbe-Grillet's presentations of passive human beings in a reified world show at least a potential for coherent understanding, and, therefore, for revolt.

Goldmann felt that the greatest living writer of themes of revolt was Jean Genet. Like Robbe-Grillet, Genet is often misunderstood. By and large, his characters are not individuals but groups. The relations between these groups involve conflict between dominators and dominated. Finally, the struggle in these plays takes place on the levels of both reality and ritual. The power of the dominators is so overwhelming in reality that the revolt of the oppressed can be successful only in ritual. This quality of Genet's plays points to another major problem faced by potential forces of criticism in modern society. In a situation in which the system is continually able to absorb revolt, to incorporate it into its growing totality—indeed, to make it profitable for the masters of the machines and organizations—critical activity is, in fact, often reduced to the level of ritual.

When Goldmann analyzed Genet's 1961 production *The Screens*, he detected a new critical dimension which went beyond the expressions of reification, the collective nature of reality, and the problems of ritual in criticism. According to Goldmann, *The Screens* was one of the first optimistic developments in avant-garde theatre. In it the dominated are able to make a successful transition from ritual to reality. They are victorious. Thus this play was "animated by faith in the possibilities of man to resist order and constraint." The world of freedom was affirmed "as something which can open up a hope for the future" (see Chapter III).

In 1966, at the end of a study of Genet, Goldmann asked, "is *The Screens* only an isolated and accidental phenomenon? Or, like the first swallow that announces the coming of Spring, does it represent a turning point in intellectual and social life?"[59] Two springs later Goldmann saw his question answered in the streets of Paris.

The events of May 1968 had a tremendous impact on Goldmann. They appeared to support not only his approach to the relationship between cultural creation and society but also his analysis of the potential forces of opposition to organizational capitalism. From the

---

58. *Ibid.*, p. 181.
59. *Ibid.*, p. 302.

time of the May "Revolution" until his death two and a half years later, Goldmann turned a large part of his attention to the development of political analyses and viable programs.

Goldmann was enthusiastic about the movements of resistance among the young in most Western societies. They were developing where he had expected them to, in the factories of higher education and training,[60] and in the large public and private bureaucracies— among the strata predicted by his analysis. And although many of these movements were confined to revolts in life style, e.g. the refusal to be "affluent" and "responsible," the desire to live in small communities, etc., he felt they represented the beginnings of a rupture in the technological totality.[61] However, Goldmann was concerned that those advanced groups and individuals who understood that the problems of modern society had to be dealt with in political as well as cultural terms were often turning to programs and organizational forms which had little relevance to the present social context and historical period.

As early as 1902, Lenin recognized that, although the theory of the revolutionary potential of the proletariat was useful, several important modifications were in order. The most significant was the realization that the routine nature of most factory tasks tends to limit the laborer's intellectual horizons. Workers generally recognize the need for collective action to end their oppression. But left to their own devices, they can develop only a trade union consciousness. Lenin's solution is well known: a well organized, highly disciplined, hierarchical party of professional revolutionaries is necessary to guide the working class away from reformism. Goldmann felt that Lenin's analysis corresponded to the reality of the contemporary historical situation to a much greater extent than did those of Luxemburg, Trotsky, or the young Lukács. Indeed, this was one of the reasons why Lenin's program was successful while each of the previously mentioned theorists was either eliminated or forced to change their position.[62] However, Lenin's solution to the problem of the

---

60. Goldmann offers an interesting hypothesis to explain the hostility of the young generation of students to the university. The university of organizational capitalism, he suggests, is becoming more and more authoritarian in order to instill discipline into future bureaucrats and technicians. This is a new function for the university, one which directly contradicts its earlier "liberating" role. The new function is necessary because the family institution has drastically changed. Traditionally, the family was the major source of discipline in the socialization process. However, it has had to become more loose, and flexible and weak in order to adopt to the needs (mobility, etc.) of advanced industrial society. See *Marxisme et sciences humaines*, pp. 353-355.

61. See the Preface to *Marxisme et sciences humaines*.

62. "Reflections on *History and Class Consciousness*," p. 77.

spontaneity of the masses raised another, perhaps even more serious, problem. The basically 'engineering' attitude of the Bolsheviks jeopardized the possibilities of socialist democracy, both within and outside the Party. The dictatorship of the vanguard of the proletariat, which Marx and Lenin had seen as a temporary expedient at most, threatened to become a permanent characteristic of socialist parties and societies.[63] In this regard, Goldmann noted that the young Lukács' hope that the Party would be internally democratized as the working class itself was transformed, turned out to be groundless.[64] In any event, Goldmann felt that, while a well disciplined, vanguard organization has had some justification in certain historical circumstances, such an organization is totally inappropriate to the quest for socialism in advanced industrial societies.

In the first place, by virtue of their training and education, the members of the new salaried middle levels have the potential to analyze their own position relative to the social whole. They are capable of understanding the political implications of their private problems. Thus Lenin's analysis of spontaneity doesn't apply to them. Goldmann thought it likely that members of the new middle stratum would experiment with new and more flexible, and democratic, organizational forms.[65]

But the differences in the needs of the traditional working class and the new middle levels imply more than variations in organizational structure. The program attached to the slogan "Workers of all countries unite!..." is no longer appropriate to the potentially revolutionary forces in modern society. The salaried middle strata *do* have something to lose by revolting against the system. Therefore it is likely that they will direct their energies within the existing society. They will attempt to modify their lives at those points where they feel most oppressed, rather than to struggle for total social transformation.

But isn't this simply a return to Bernsteinian reformism? A continued support for, and even defense of, traditional bourgeois property and authority relations? Goldmann thought not. Because, for reasons mentioned earlier, mere economic reforms, getting a bigger share of the same old pie, will no longer buy off the new middle strata. They are going to demand reforms which will of necessity get to the very heart of the capitalist system. Goldmann felt the new middle strata would demand nothing less than the complete democratization of their workplaces: self-management. This is the essence of

---

63. See, *Marxisme et sciences humaines*, p. 306.
64. "Reflections on *History and Class Consciousness*," p. 77.
65. See *Marxisme et sciences humaines*, esp. p. 358 for Goldmann's discussion of some of the organizational lessons of May 1968.

Goldmann's conception of revolutionary-reformism: the idea that political revolution will occur *after* economic transformations have been accomplished. Although this contradicts the thesis of *State and Revolution*, Goldmann noted that it did find precedent in several bourgeois revolutions in Europe.

Thus he wrote in 1969, "We can thus see the possibility of a transformation on a model very different both from that of a political revolution of the proletariat which precedes the transformation of the economy and from the partial and limited reformism of the Western social democrats whose aim was simply the improvement of existing capitalist society, but which bears a considerable resemblance to the development of the bourgeoisie inside feudal society; in this latter case the seizure of economic power and a great increase in the social importance of the rising class *preceded* the seizure of political power, which was, moreover, depending on the country involved, at first revolutionary in nature (England, France), but also subsequently, evolutionary and reformist (Germany, Italy). This is precisely what is nowadays called the revolutionary-reformist analysis, which links the ideas I have been outlining with the equally important idea of self-management" [emphasis in original].[66] Goldmann was well aware that 19th century Germany and Italy could not have had their reformist transformation if England and France had not first had their revolutions. And he realized it was likely that the first moves to self-management in capitalist societies[67] would probably be violent. In this sense the struggles of May 1968 were perhaps an indication of how the early self-management revolution might occur. And Goldmann felt that one of the major lessons to be learned from 1968 was the importance of some kind of organization to guide the movement of revolutionary-reform. While it was clear that neither the institutional Marxist parties of the Second and Third Internationals nor the organizations and tactics of the third world revolutionaries were adequate to this task, it was equally obvious to him that the extremely loose organizations which emerged among students and young workers were also inappropriate.

In his final months Goldmann became more and more convinced of the enduring value of Marx's and Luxemburg's assessments of the

---

66. "Reflections on *History and Class Consciousness*," p. 82.
67. The idea of self-management was developed in Yugoslavia in order to provide an alternate political structure to that of the Soviet Union and Peoples' Democracies. In spite of the fact that the Yugoslavian economy was too primitive to allow for a large scale decentralization of economic and political authority, the experiment in self-management worked well among the skilled technicians. See "Reflections on *History and Class Consciousness*," p. 81. For a critical account see Svetozar Stojanovic, *Between Ideals and Reality* (New York: Oxford, 1973) pp. 115-134.

alternatives confronting developed capitalism. The historical choice is still between barbarism and socialism. The most critical tasks confronting progressive thinkers, Goldmann felt, are the development of programs and organizations to facilitate the transition to self-management and socialist democracy.

There are striking similarities between the contributions of Lukács in the period from 1908 to 1926 and the lifework of his disciple Lucien Goldmann. Like Lukács, Goldmann maintained and elaborated the dialectical heritage of Hegel and Marx. Moreover, like the Lukács of *The Soul and the Forms* and the *Theory of the Novel*, he left a body of valuable concrete research in the sociology of culture.

But, Goldmann shared many of his mentor's weaknesses. These go beyond the fact that both men had a penchant for the best of bourgeois culture or that both saw middle class salaried workers and intellectuals—like themselves—as the carriers of revolutionary faith and saviors of humanity. The major problem, in this respect, is that the social and political analyses of both Lukács and Goldmann have proved to be inadequate.

Five years after Goldmann's death, it is by no means clear that the standard of living of the middle level strata will continue to rise, as Goldmann predicted and made fundamental to his analysis. Nor is it certain, in light of continuing international monetary crises, increasing unemployment throughout the capitalist world, and the interesting new phenomenon of "stagflation," that capitalism has succeeded in "fine-tuning" its economy. This, of course, doesn't mean that global capitalism won't temporarily restabilize itself in the more or less near future. It does mean, however, that along with most of the other mass society theorists, Goldmann was premature in accepting the neo-Keynesian mythology of a fully rationalized and controlled capitalist market.

A further problem with Goldmann's analysis is the issue of the indispensibility to the economy of highly trained and educated technicians and bureaucrats. The past half decade has witnessed the development of a worker surplus in virtually all areas of the salaried middle levels. To many of these skilled workers the idea of guaranteed job security for advanced educational training has become a bad joke. Indeed, it is apparent that many among Goldmann's new middle strata are beginning to experience the same insecurity and relative pauperization Marx predicted for the traditional working classes. Once again, this does not mean that the employment situation will not improve or that highly skilled and educated labor will not continue to become a proportionally more important component of the overall work force. However, it does show that *all* workers, whether they are unskilled or hold Ph.D.'s, will remain subject to the vicissitudes of an essentially irrational capitalist economy.

Some of these developments were the result of factors beyond the potential consciousness of the early 1960's. For example, it would have been difficult to recognize the ecological and political issues involved in the so-called "energy crisis" from that historical location. But the failure of capitalist economies to become fully rationalized and managed, the growing surplus of middle level salaried workers and the threat to their standards of living, continuing inflation, the crisis in public services, etc. were foreseen by a number of Goldmann's contemporaries.[68] In fact, there were theorists whom Goldmann rightly criticized as being rigid, dogmatic and unimaginative[69] who, in retrospect, provided a better picture of capitalist economic development than Goldmann did.

Yet notwithstanding the problems with some of his later social and political analyses, many of the writers who were closer to the actual developments of modern capitalism than Goldmann were less perceptive than he in terms of the ability to carry out imaginative research and to appreciate the philosophical foundations of the dialectical method. The fact that in the early 1960's Goldmann could reject the abandoning of critical Marxism by the Frankfurt School is a tribute to his mastery of the dialectic of contradiction and possibility. However, his vision of the historical totality suffered from its own form of one-dimensionality. Goldmann was fond of Pascal's observation that he could never finish writing a manuscript without the feeling that it had finally reached the point where it should be starting. This is the feeling one gets while reading much of Goldmann's wórk. Although it is finished, something is missing. Part of this is due, of course, of the normal dialectic between a work and its changing historical environment. But the major source of this incompetence is Goldmann's failure to extend the dialectical orientation to matters of economic analysis.

Georg Lukács, whose early works captured Goldmann's imagination almost a decade after Lukács himself rejected them, outlived his disciple by eight months. Goldmann died on October 2, 1970. His premature death was doubly tragic in that it came just at the time that a new critical Marxism was returning to questions of art and the cultural superstructure. The revival of interest in the aesthetic analyses of the Frankfurt School and the writings of Antonio Gramsci

---

68. See, for example, Ernest Mandel's "Where is America Going?" *New Left Review* 54 (March-April 1969), pp. 3-15.

69. *Marxisme et sciences humaines*, p. 316.

on cultural hegemony and the function of intellectuals, for example, has focused attention on many of the issues Goldmann dealt with. He could have contributed substantially to the current dialogue. As things stand, the essays which follow, and for that matter Goldmann's work in general, should not be read and judged as a completed system of sociology or of cultural analysis. Rather, they are best seen, along with the writings of Adorno, Horkheimer, Marcuse, and Gramsci, among others, as part of a larger effort to sustain and elaborate one of the most fruitful dimensions of the Marxian tradition.

William W. Mayrl

1. THE IMPORTANCE OF THE CONCEPT OF POTENTIAL CONSCIOUSNESS FOR COMMUNICATION*

For about twenty years, I as well as others have grappled with the concept of potential consciousness [*conscience possible*]. I have always regarded this concept from a psychological and sociological viewpoint; but it also seems to me to have great importance on the plane of communication and information transmission. Since I am unfamiliar with the problems of information theory and cybernetics, however, it would be difficult for me to present the concept in that perspective. Thus I will restrict my analysis to what in my opinion constitutes Marx's most fruitful discovery, and remains both the center of contemporary Marxist thought and one of the principal operative concepts for the study of society. I emphasize, moreover, that as in psychology we use the concept of potential consciousness in a way which is ultimately more empirical than methodical; and that even if we have some orienting ideas, we are far from having specified the concept sufficiently to permit a collective endeavor in which everyone would know exactly what rules to apply. When I formed a research group in the sociology of literature at Brussels, I was asked: What grid do you use? But we have no grid, which is precisely what makes the work difficult.

I have translated a familiar term in German Marxist literature, *Zugerechte Bewusstsein*, as "potential consciousness." Literally, it can be translated as the consciousness "ascribed" [*conscience calculée*] to some social group by the researcher, sociologist, or

*Originally published in *Le concept d'information dans la science contemporaine* (Paris: Cahiers de Royaumont, Editions de Minuit, 1965).

economist.[1] In a famous passage in *The Holy Family*, for example, Marx referred to this concept, explaining that the question is not what this or that proletarian thinks or even what the proletarians as a whole think, but is instead the consciousness of the proletarian class.[2] This is the great distinction between *real* and *potential* consciousness.

Briefly, the problem is that a conversation—or, in what I suppose is the colloquium's language, a transmission of information—involves not only a man or a device emitting information and a mechanism transmitting it, but also a human being somewhere who receives it. Even if the path is very long and detours through a chain of devices and machines, at the end of the chain there is always a human being whose consciousness, we know, can in no way "overlook" what is important.

By virtue of its very structure, this receiving consciousness is opaque to an entire information series which thus is not received; whereas other information is received, or is received in a distorted way. In fact, those who consider the situation externally and try to compare what was emitted with what was received often find that only a part of the information sent has been received, and that at the level of reception even this part has acquired a meaning rather different from what was sent.

At issue here is an extremely important fact which tends particularly to call into question all contemporary sociology insofar as it is centered more on the concept of *real* consciousness than on that of potential consciousness. In its descriptive methods, its methods of inquiry, this sociology is in fact interested only in what people actually think. But—I have often cited this example—supposing one used methods a thousand times more accurate than those at our disposal today, the most precise possible inquiry into Russian peasants in January 1917 would probably have found that the great majority were loyal to the Tsar and did not even envisage the possibility of overthrowing the monarchy. Yet by the end of the year, this real consciousness of the peasants had changed radically on that point.

Thus the problem is to know not what a group thinks, but what

---

1. This German term is usually translated as "imputed" or "ascribed" consciousness. See Karl Marx and Friedrich Engels, *The Holy Family*, tr. R. Dixon (Moscow: Foreign Languages Publishing House, 1956), pp. 52-53; Georg Lukács, *History and Class Consciousness*, tr. Rodney Livingstone (London: Merlin Press, 1971), pp. xviii-xix, 51, and translator's note on pp. 344-345; and István Mészaros, "Contingent and Necessary Class Consciousness" in Mészaros, ed., *Aspects of "History and Class Consciousness"* (London: Routledge & Kegan Paul, 1971, p. 94 [*Trans.*].

2. Marx and Engels, *op. cit.*, p. 53 [*Trans.*].

changes are likely to occur in its consciousness in the absence of modification in the group's essential nature.

In fact, in several months the information transmitted to and received by the peasants about the Russian social structure and the possibilities of changing it had transformed their consciousness. At the same time, however, for reasons which I will analyze later (I have not chosen this example accidentally), the Russian revolutionaries had been led to modify entirely the traditional socialist position on a particularly important point. And they did so beginning from the analysis of the concept of the possibility of transmitting information.

Until then all socialist thought, or at least all the theoreticians with any authority in the socialist movement, had agreed that socialism had to oppose individual property in land and promote large scale state or cooperative cultivation. Lenin was a political man, but on this question he did the work of a sociologist or even an information theorist. Lenin explained that while a certain number of socialist slogans could be transmitted to the peasants, they could never be made to understand the advantages of large-scale cultivation or be convinced that they should renounce all claims to private ownership of land. Despite their loyalty to the Tsar, an information series tending to change their consciousness could be transmitted to them. But there was one message they could never be made to assimilate: that it would be better to work cooperatively than to possess land by personal right. To the indignation of many socialists, including Rosa Luxemburg, Lenin formulated a new and entirely unexpected slogan: the land to the peasants. This is a classic example of sociological analysis based on the concept of potential consciousness.

It is important for those who want to intervene in social life to know which information can be transmitted in a given situation, which will undergo more or less significant distortions in reception, and which cannot be received.

In a rather empirical way I want to propose four stages of analysis in the study of this problem which it is important not to confuse. In the first place, very often information is not received due to a lack of previous information. Since I am not a professional mathematician, if you show me a particularly complex mathematical formula I will not understand much; thus I will have to be furnished a further information series so that I can understand the message. For psychologists and sociologists this is the least interesting case. Unfortunately certain researchers, especially among philosophers examining problems of dialogue, often think that all misunderstandings originally arise from such insufficient information, and that it suffices to be honest and to give the partner all the needed pieces of information so that reception can occur under favorable conditions. In reality, there are reception problems at other levels and transmission difficulties unrelated to the insufficiency of previous information.

A second stage, more important but still not properly sociological, is that of individual psychic structure. Freud illuminated the existence of an entire series of structural elements of desires and aversions resulting from the individual's biography, making his conscious ego impermeable to some information and making it distort the meaning of other information. In this case, if the information is to be received a transformation of consciousness must be affected on a purely psychological plane, without any social change. Here the obstacle to communication is more resistant than in the former case; but a possibility of surmounting it can still be imagined. An individual psychic structure can be transformed at its boundaries: the milieu in which the individual lives can be changed, he can be made to undergo psychoanalytic treatment, etc.

A third stage, sociological but still peripheral, is that in which, given the structure of its *real* consciousness resulting from its past and from the multiple events which have influenced it, a particular social group of individuals resists receiving certain information. For example, we could imagine that scholars attached to a scientific school and to a thesis they have defended might refuse to recognize some new theory which would call all their earlier work into question. Even at this stage, however, the problem is still not fundamental. A great number of misunderstandings and difficulties in dialogue occur at this level; but I think such a group of scholars can continue as a group even if it becomes aware of the relative value of its theories. Ultimately, it can integrate the new theory. Here, it is still a matter of a possible transformation of real consciousness which does not place the group's existence in question.

Now we come to a level more important to the present area of concern, where the problem of what Marx called the limits of potential consciousness occurs. In this case, to effect transmission the group as such must disappear, or else must be transformed to the point of losing its essential social characteristics.

In brief, there can be information whose transmission is incompatible with the fundamental characteristics of some social group. Such information transcends the group's maximum potential consciousness. The sociologist studying a social group must always inquire about the fundamental intellectual categories, the *specific* aspect of the concepts of space, time, good, evil, history, causality, and so forth, which structure its consciousness. He must ask to what extent these categories are linked with its existence, what horizons [*limites*] of the field of consciousness they give rise to, and finally, what information lies beyond these horizons and cannot be received without fundamental social transformation.

In fact, every group tends to have an adequate knowledge of reality; but its knowledge can extend only up to a maximum horizon compatible with its existence. Beyond this horizon, information can be received only if the group's structure is transformed, exactly as in the case of individual obstacles where information can be received only if the individual's psychic structure is transformed.

At issue here is a fundamental concept for studying the possibilities of comunication in social life. It has great operative importance, but at present it is insufficiently studied and procedures for its use are still barely elucidated.

I want to insist that in the study of human phenomena we never deal with problems located uniquely on the plane of consciousness. Actually, every social or individual human fact occurs as an *overall* [*global*] effort of a subject to adapt to a surrounding world. It is a process oriented toward a state of equilibrium; it remains provisional insofar as it will be modified by the subject's active transformation of the surrounding world within this equilibrium, and simultaneously by the extension of the sphere of that action. Under these conditions, any attempt to separate a particular domain of this equilibration process can be a useful procedure for comprehension and research, provided it remains provisional and is later corrected by inserting the object studied into the major relevant ensembles of which it is part.

These considerations seem important to the extent that the links between the social group's structure and the difficulties of information transmission are of two different types. Difficulty may result from the fact that the information transcends the categorial frameworks structuring the group's collective consciousness. In this case the difficulty results from the incompatibility, so to speak, between the elements of the structuration which, if not permanent, are still relatively durable, and the nature of the message transmitted.

The life of men and social groups is not a state but always an ensemble of processes. Transmission problems may result from the functioning of this process, which is always linked mediately or immediately to the individual or collective subject's tendency to maintain its structure and to act in the direction of equilibration. But here the relative, provisional character of any separation becomes especially important. The difficulty of transmitting information may result not only from its conflict with the behavior of the sector studied, but also from its conflict with the repercussions which this sector's functioning may have on processes unfolding in another sector which the research has provisionally eliminated.

Let's pause for a few examples. The history of the physical and social sciences can be presented as an ensemble of purely intellectual processes. This way of framing the object can be extremely useful from the scientific viewpoint. Sociologists must never forget, however, that every scientific theory has practical social consequences, even though the researcher who elaborated it may never have considered them and may be completely ignorant of them. But, especially in the human sciences, if at a given moment these practical consequences threaten to conflict with the practical aims of a social group, the ramifications affect the theory's elaboration as much as the possibilities of its being discussed once it is elaborated—that is, they affect the transmission of the message.

Likewise, men's action on other men can be provisionally distinguished from their action on the external world. Again, it must not be forgotten that these two forms of action react on each other: that every transformation of the surrounding world entails a transformation of the individual or collective subject, and inversely.

In the same way, the distinction between subjective and objective elements in information is undeniably important; but it, too, has only a relative value. For the psychosociologist, even the most valorizing or most discordant subjective element constitutes an *objective* reality as a psychosocial fact. Inversely, even the most rigorous statement occurs within a consciousness and is thus a *subjective* fact linked to an equilibration process which is oriented toward a goal.

A last example is especially important for the conditions in which messages are elaborated and transmitted. The life of society does not form a homogeneous whole; it is composed of partial groups whose interrelations are multiple and complex. Overall, they could be schematically defined as an ensemble of conflicts and collabora- tions. But the life of each group constitutes an ensemble of processes oriented toward a specific equilibrium; consequently, a group of specific, particular values will structure the conscious sector of these processes. Even if the awareness of certain information conforms to the mental categories of the group's consciousness and favors the equilibrium toward which it is oriented, it can have highly detrimental consequences for the realization of that equilibrium if it is also produced in the consciousness of other constituent social groups in society. But bad faith is an individual phenomenon found only very exceptionally and temporarily in extremely restricted social groups. Thus, such situations give rise not to acts of bad faith but to ideological phenomena, to considerable distortions in the elaboration, transmission, and reception of certain information.

Having said this, and reiterating the purely empirical character of the rules we can outline today for using the concept of maximum potential consciousness, I want to conclude by enumerating three particularly important principles.

1) Today, the elaboration and transmission of information about physiochemical and even biological nature is in an essentially different situation from information about psychological, social, and moral life. In the first case, the desire to master nature constitutes a universal element structuring the ensemble of intellectual processes of almost all existing social groups—in any case, all social groups in moderately and highly advanced industrial societies. Thus, the same physics, or at least a very similar one, is done in Washington, Moscow, Tokyo, Paris, and Warsaw. In this domain, the difficulties in transmitting messages fall under the first and third rubrics in this initial classification, and are very rarely related to the fourth—to maximum potential consciousness. Of course, physiochemical thought does not seem to me independent of the physical and intellectual structure of man and the universe. On an imaginary planet inhabited by beings who could not move in space but could act psychically on colors, change of color—and not change of space, as for human consciousness—would constitute the operative, quantitative principle. These beings could not call one space twice as large as another; instead, they would call a certain blue twice as large as a certain red (if repeating the action which produced the first resulted in reproducing the second).

But for men living on our planet, a scientific objectivity is being constituted for everything concerning the physiochemical sciences. Without being competent in this regard, it seems to me that the same is true for the natural sciences, although to a less advanced degree. When human facts are in question, however, conscious or non-conscious ends become specific. Thus, for the reasons I have mentioned, the structure of consciousness requires that certain messages be developed and transmitted, that others be distorted, and that the elaboration and transmission of whole series of messages conflicting with the realization of those ends be obstructed. Of course, these three categories of information do not coincide from one group to another, which indicates the extreme complexity involved in studying the transmission of messages bearing on the different aspects of men's life.

2) One of the most important rules for extracting essential social structures and constructing the concept of maximum potential consciousness in each concrete case is founded on the initial hypothesis that all human facts constitute processes of meaningful

structuration oriented toward provisional, dynamic equilibrations. But human facts are initially given to us not in this form, but as a mass of partial givens which can be empirically verified and enumerated but whose structure is very difficult to isolate. Thus, after doing our research as honestly as possible, if we do not obtain such a structure and the object studied does not become meaningful, then we must admit that it is poorly delineated [*découpé*].

If a student came to see me and said that he wanted to do a project on "hierarchy" or "dictatorship," I would reply that neither "hierarchy" nor "dictatorship" exists as a meaningful structure. There are *hierarchies* and groups of hierarchies of a similar type—just as there are groups of dictatorships—which are meaningful. This is true, for example, of the group of post-revolutionary dictatorships, and of other types which are social realities.

Insofar as they lead us to study objects which are not meaningful structures, general delineations like "hierarchy" and "dictatorship" as such lack operative value. The object must be framed so that it can be studied as the destructuration of a traditional structure and the rise of a new one. To use a philosophical term, I believe the Hegelian and Marxist concept of the passage from quantity to quality denotes simply the instant in becoming when a structure's internal transformations eliminate the old structure and give rise to a new one, which is subsequently oriented toward a new state of equilibrium.

Perhaps the concepts of comprehension and explication can be specified here. The description of a meaningful structure and its internal bonds is a phenomenon of *comprehension*. But of course we are always confronted with a relative structure composed of partial structures, which itself forms part of more comprehensive structures: therefore the attempt to describe the more comprehensive structure's development helps to explicate the structure incorporated [*englobée*] in it. If I study Pascal's *Pensées* as an internally meaningful structure I try to comprehend them; but if I then insert them as a partial structure into the broader structure of the Jansenist movement I *comprehend* Jansenism and *explicate* Pascal's *Pensées* by Jansenism. If I insert the Jansenist movement into the overall structure of the *noblesse de robe*, I *comprehend* the history of the *noblesse de robe* and *explicate* the genesis of Jansenism by it. Then if I perform the same operation with the *noblesse de robe* in 17th century France, I place myself on the level of explication for the *noblesse de robe* and on the level of comprehension for the overall structure.

The use of this procedure accords a privileged value to equilibration processes oriented not toward certain partial ends, but toward the overall organization of mutual relations among men and of relations between men an nature. It constitutes a primary rule in the attempt to distinguish the genesis and limits of maximum potential consciousness in each concrete case.

3) The final point concerns a particular area of research in which lies my own experience and that of a certain number of Marxist historians. I want to point out that philosophical, literary, and artistic works prove to have particular value for sociology because they approximate the maximum potential consciousness of those privileged social groups whose mentality, thought, and behavior are oriented toward an overall world view.

If these works have a privileged value not only for research but for men in general, it is because they correspond to what the essential groups tend toward: to the maximum potential consciousness accessible to them. Inversely, for the same reason, the study of these works is one of the most effective ways (but not the sole or even the best way) of understanding the structure of a group's consciousness, the consciousness of a group and the maximum correspondence to reality it can attain.

For example, analyzing rationalist incomprehension of tragic thought—concretely, analyzing the common elements in Voltaire's and Valéry's reactions to Pascal's work—enables us to grasp, at different moments of its history, the limits of a social group's incomprehension of a certain type of message originating in another group.

These brief, schematic remarks on the concept of maximum potential consciousness are, I believe, an approach to one of the most important conceptual instruments for the study of social life in general and of message transmission in particular. To be scientific, sociologists must ask not merely what some member of a social group thinks today about refrigerators and gadgets or about marriage and sexual life, but what is the field of consciousness within which some group can vary its ways of thinking about all these problems without modifying its structure. In short, the inquiry concerns the horizons which a group's consciousness of reality cannot overcome without a profound social transformation.

The concept of potential consciousness leads to the center of the problems of comprehending social life. Even though we have prepared some methodological rudiments for its use, a great deal still remains to be done in clarifying these problems.

2. POSSIBILITIES OF CULTURAL ACTION
THROUGH THE MASS MEDIA*

The organizers of this conference have requested a contribution from a researcher whose activity has been devoted mainly to cultural creation rather than to its effect on the public. I think they were hoping for remarks on the fundamental conditions for that effect in contemporary industrial societies, rather than precise remarks on any particular aspect of the mass media's operation which could result only from concrete, specific research.

Let me begin with some unquestionably simplistic thinking about this problem of fundamental conditions. This thinking, often found in the press and even in some analyses with scientific pretensions, has an initial appearance of validity. Here I would like to develop some remarks in connection with it. It can be said that recent social transformations in Western industrial societies have considerably diminished social crises in these societies (with the important but not fundamental exception of the Black problem in the U.S.A.). At the same time, these transformations have increased both the professional skills required of the great majority of those who participate in active life in any way, and also the possibilities of assuring that skill through the rising standard of living and the shortening of work time. More simply: in Western industrial

*This paper was delivered at the international seminar on *"Mass-media" et création imaginaire* sponsored by the Institut de Sociologie de l'Art (Faculté des Lettres de Tours) and the Association Internationale pour la liberté de la Culture, fondation C.I.N.I., in Venice, October 1967.

societies, nominal and real income have increased over the last ten years; and, despite the considerable increase in production, the progress of productivity has allowed schooling and apprenticeship to be prolonged. At the same time, high school and university diplomas have gained increasingly decisive importance for the ultimate social position to which individuals can aspire and for their future standard of living. This results simultaneously in a considerable increase in the length of schooling, a rise in the level of instruction, and an increase in the mass of information transmitted in one way or another to most of the members of these societies.

In this process, a distinctive position is occupied by the mass media: from radio and television, now constituent elements of the life style of most Europeans and Americans; to the cinema, transmitting both information and imaginative works which sometimes have real aesthetic value; to that well-distributed modern encyclopedia, the paperback book, and that schematic or stereotyped degradation of imaginary narrative, the comic strip.

On the basis of these considerations it is possible to sketch an optimistic picture of an uninterrupted rise in the cultural level of society as a whole which has good chances of continuing into the future. Of course, it must be added that all progress of this kind entails both an increase in the number of people actually having access to culture, and a corresponding growth of the much larger fringe which remains at the level of what can be called a pseudo-culture (which, nonetheless, constitutes a sort of antechamber of genuine culture).

There are many more people today who have heard of and read Racine, Montaigne, and even Goethe and Shakespeare than there were in the last century. Correlatively, of course, there are many more who read romance magazines today than read popular pseudo-literature in the last century. But for the most part, the children of these latter readers are likely to enter the category of consumers of genuine culture.

To make this picture more exact one can also mention the conservative, traditional character of scholarly institutions. They still preserve many traits of the age in which they were reserved for privileged strata and constituted a way of conserving and perpetuating their privileges. It can also be stated that the mass media, which sprang up spontaneously and planlessly, retain many traces of this original improvisation which prevent their true adaptation to modern civilization.

Finally, one can give the impression of a critical, progressive attitude by insisting on the need to struggle against these privileges and to adapt the organization of the mass media to the "democratic" requirements of industrial societies.

But this analysis seems both superficial and deeply tainted by apologetic ideology. It is ignorant of, and usually ignores, the fundamental aspect of the problem of communication. The transmission of an ensemble of knowledge depends not only on the quantity of information emitted or even on its nature (a particularly serious problem in modern societies). Additionally and primarily, it depends on what can be technically called the structure of the receiver, which in the present case is constituted by the mental and psychic structure of the individuals who attend schools, listen to the radio, watch television, go to the movies, and read paperbacks or comic strips. Here I cannot develop an epistemological analysis of the nature of cognitive phenomena ranging from perception and everyday thought to scientific thought and cultural creation. I would merely stress that, on the one hand, all these forms of cognitive activity are mediately or immediately linked to individual and social praxis; and that, on the other hand, they are constituted by the relation of a multiplicity of sense data and the active creation of an invariant. (This invariant is provisional and changes in the course of historical development. Examples are *objects* of perception, *principles of conservation* or *reversible structures* for scientific thought, *world views* for cultural creation, etc.). In other words, these forms of cognitive activity incorporate a synthesis of receptive passivity and organizing activity.

But the rise of recent forms of Western industrial societies—called organizational capitalism [*capitalisme d'organisation*], consumer society, mass society, etc.—has considerably strengthened and even qualitatively changed a process which had already begun to be manifest in liberal and monopoly capitalism. This process threatens to perpetuate and intensify itself in the future, entailing substantial modification of men's psychic structure in our societies.

Of course, I cannot outline a history of men's psychic structure in Western culture here. I will suffice to contrast European liberal society up to 1914—the period in which traditional bourgeois culture reached its zenith—with the present situation. The period between the last two wars, an era of great social and economic upheavals which had profound repercussions on intellectual life (the era of existentialism's rise and development), can nonetheless be considered transitional.

We are familiar with the critical analysis of the structure of consciousness and cultural creation in liberal and monopoly capitalist society developed by Marx and Marxist thinkers (especially Lukács): the well-known theory of reification. Restricting the discussion to some central ideas, we can say that the entire social structure, the global character of interhuman relations, tends to disappear from the consciousness of individuals. Thus the sphere in which their synthesizing activity can be manifested is considerably reduced; and an individualistic, atomized vision of men's relations with other men and with the universe is created. Community, positive values, the hope of transcendence [*dépassement*] and all qualitative structures tend to disappear from men's consciousness, yielding to the faculty of understanding [*l'entendement*] and the quantitative. Reality loses all transparency and becomes opaque; man becomes limited and disoriented. The considerable progress of the productive forces, and concomitantly of science and technology, is realized only at the price of an enormous narrowing of the field of consciousness, especially in regard to man's possibilities and the nature of his relations with others.

This critique seems rigorous; yet today the period it bears on appears retrospectively as one of substantial cultural creation, even aside from technical and scientific progress. This is not, of course, a result of masking the shadow zones, the misery of the proletariat and the popular strata which Marx and socialist thinkers illuminated so perspicaciously and abundantly. But it remains true that, among other forms, there was a great literary form, "the novel" of the problematic hero, arising from precisely the traits analyzed by the theories of reification dealing with commercial and 19th century liberal capitalism. The novel form was founded precisely on the opacity of social life and the individual's difficulty in orienting himself and giving his life meaning.

Moreover, this form has a special status in the history of cultural creation. It narrates the degraded quest of a hero seeking values he is not conscious of, in a society which ignores or has lost nearly all memory of them. The novel was perhaps the first great literary form predominant in any social order to have an essentially critical nature, and to be unable to admit of either a positive hero or a corresponding philosophy. Judging and criticizing society according to the values of the development of the individual and the personality, which society explicitly extols but whose realization it actually prevents, the novel preserves the link with values of transcendence, even if only in the form of absence. On the other hand, the individualist philosophy developed in different forms during the same era (rationalism, empiricism, Enlightenment philosophy) renounced the categories of transcendence and totality, and was never subsequently accompanied by a corresponding literary creation. The outlines I have sketched thus conserve all the central ideas of the analysis of reification, but give them a different meaning. Where Marx and the first Marxists accented the negative aspects, today we see a powerful intellectual creativity and a reality which was positive in some respects.

And what was this creativity based on? Continuing to reflect on the problematic novel, we encounter this basis. Individualism, and the explicit requirement of individual and personality development, are manifested through the hero's obscure quest, which terminates in the awareness that it is impossible to end the quest or to give life meaning.

Moving from literary creation to social reality, we must point out that, from a simultaneously cultural and social viewpoint, liberal society was characterized by a relatively large stratum of notables (giving this term a sociological meaning which includes both the notables of recognized social status, who were props of the dominant classes, and the notables of the opposition, the cadres of workers' parties and trade unions). Sociologically, the existence of this stratum of notables was undoubtedly grounded in the economy: in the many small businesses whose directors could hardly comprehend social and economic life in its entirety. In a situation where they had to make hazardous decisions of utmost importance to their survival, they had to gather around themselves a more or less extensive group of advisors linked to the business either directly (administrative staffs) or externally (lawyers, notaries, etc.). Socially this stratum, which was the base of parliamentary democracy, also constituted an intermediary between the urgencies which actually decided matters of general interest and the mass of functionaries [*exécutants*].

Thus in the society Marx and his disciples analyzed, somewhere in the interplay of interferences between the hierarchical organization of business and the democratic organization of the market and political life, there was a social structure in which an important autonomy of individual consciousness persisted despite the process of reification discussed above. This autonomy was founded on the more or less extensive responsibilities with which nearly every individual was charged: from the skilled worker's anxiety about finding a job, doing his work well, and guaranteeing his family's existence; to the decisions which peasants and members of the middle classes had to make every day; to the increasingly numerous responsibilities which bourgeois notables and political leaders of society had to assume. That is, there was a psychic and intellectual structure in liberal society which permitted the organization of a public opinion functioning as significantly in political and social life as in cultural life.

However, a radical social transformation developed in Western industrial societies (to which I confine my discussion, not being familiar with Soviet society), through the intermediate state of monopoly capitalism, its corresponding social and economic crises, and the existential philosophy and literature bound up with these crises (WWI, 1918-1923 revolutionary crisis in Germany, 1929-1933 economic crisis, Nazism, WWII, and, on the periphery of the industrialized societies, Italian fascism, the Spanish Civil War, and the Franco regime). Of course this transformation cannot be analyzed here in detail; but one of its most important consequences was the suppression of the particular stratum I have called "notables" in the broad sense. Consequently, there was a radical transformation of the nature and functions of public opinion.

Basically, leaving aside the Asian cultures corresponding to what Marx called the Asiatic mode of production, this may be the first time in Western history that the social order has been oriented toward (without having reached) a structuration founded in principle on a dichotomy, which tends to intensify and become total, between a considerable mass of individuals whose incomes are relatively high but who are totally passive, and a small group of technocrats (in different economic, social, and political domains) who tend to monopolize all decisions.

It must be emphasized that this transformation is radical and qualitative, not merely the emergence of a new form of dominant/dominated class opposition continuing those in the West since the beginning of historical time. The difference lies in the fact that the social equilibria historically realized by dominant classes were always involuntary, pragmatic, and therefore extremely unstable. In fact, whatever the degree of oppression and violence on which they were established, they were always based on an *active* equilibration of the dominated strata: on their temporary participation in and acceptance of the established order, even if this participation was mainly implicit and relatively little evidenced in political consciousness.

These equilibria were unstable, and could last only as long as there was a correspondence between the particular equilibrations of the dominated groups and the equilibrium which the dominant class imposed on the whole society. Consequently, systems of unstable equilibrium periodically appeared at more or less brief intervals. Marx designated these as conflicts between the productive forces and the relations of production: conflicts which led to the transformation of the established social order.

It has often been said that the development of capitalist society, insofar as it introduced an element of conscious, rational planning into a spontaneous and more or less pragmatic progression, represented an essential advance in European historical development. But this statement must immediately be tempered with the fact that, in liberal as well as monopoly capitalism, such rationalization operated only in businesses and not in national or world production as a whole. That is, the spontaneity of the equilibration (and, implicitly, the psychic activity of the subjects on which it was founded) was considerably reduced at the level of the working class, especially after rationatization and assembly line work. But this spontaneity remained extremely strong, even growing stronger at the level of the notables. Even at the level of workers it was preserved in an important sector of their behavior: private and family life.

Contemporary organizational capitalism has discovered, elaborated, and adjusted mechanisms of economic and even social self-regulation which have allowed almost uninterrupted economic vitality and considerable development of productive forces since WWII. But what characterizes organizational capitalism and opposes it to liberal or even monopoly capitalism is that to a relatively advanced degree it has introduced conscious, rational action even at the level of production as a whole (national and, up to a point, European production); but that in so doing it has succeeded in reducing almost every active function of the great mass of its functionaries to a degree previously unknown in the West.

The State itself has changed its nature. Participating directly or indirectly in production, it tends to be modeled on the hierarchical structure of production, whereas the aim of the self-regulation mechanisms is to make possible and even probable the spontaneous perpetuation of harmony among the individual equilibrations in the life of the functionaries, and in the whole dynamic equilibration. As I have already said, these mechanisms succeed in their aim, enabled by the present level of technique to link the development of society to a rise in the functionaries' standard of living. No doubt, this rise is weaker than general technical progress; but it is real nonetheless.

Almost all sociologists understand the dialectical process by which this situation leads the administrative apparatus of production and the State to intervene through consumption, even into individuals' private lives. At the same time, individuals develop the tendency to passively accept and even to welcome this intervention.

Clearly, the rise of a social organization in which most members are fundamentally passive constitutes a considerable danger, not only for the elaboration but also for the reception and assimilation of cultural creations. For centuries, cultural life in most human societies has been founded on an enormous ferment of micro-activities of all the members of society. Especially in the West, it has been founded on the particularly intense activity of the crystallizing ferments which have served as frameworks (in the broad sense of the word). Today this cultural life is gravely menaced by the contemporary evolution of industrial societies.

Thus in the evolution of modern societies there is a growing danger of what I would call a deculturalization through the disorganization of the receivers: a primary "jamming" in what I would call the cultural circuit. In traditional societies, these receivers once constituted an integrated reception system.

In addition, if the considerably increased quantity of information in all domains which the mass media transmit is to be assimilated, it requires a particularly powerful synthesizing activity—but at a time when, as I have said, social evolution diminishes the intensity of this activity. That is, even without every tendentious distortion by state and pressure group interests, by itself the mass of information bombarding a relatively passive receiver can be disorienting and can enfeeble comprehension.

It is essential always to bear in mind that there are two ways to read a book, to see a film, or to receive information. There is a passive reception which submits to the information, and an active reception which seeks in the book or film an invitation to reflection, a problem which has to be assimilated, a voice of privileged importance in discussing life's great problems—a voice which integrates information in a global vision, perfecting or modifying that vision.

Also, the real problem of cultural action and the development of personal character in modern societies lies at the level of economic and social life and its transformation. The problem is the possibilities of reorienting this life toward a renaissance of activity and of individual responsibility.

From many directions and especially in socialist thought, a relatively new idea has appeared on this plane which could establish the fundamental perspective for all who remain attached to humanism and to the cultural progress of our countries: economic democracy and self-management. It must be acknowledged, however, that this entails a decrease in productive efficiency. The problem then becomes one of knowing if there are still ways to make this an acceptable price, not enormous but nonetheless real, in Western industrial societies. It must be paid, however, to safeguard two values which today are more intimately and inseparably linked than ever before: culture and freedom.

This is the fundamental problem; but the schema outlined here must be retouched and some comments must be added. First, the corrections. It goes without saying that technocratic society, which needs increasingly skilled specialists even on the plane of execution, can neither completely stupefy its members nor render them entirely passive. Professional skill is one domain where a rather high minimal level of intellectual life remains absolutely essential to the functioning of society. The rulers of technocratic societies are faced with the difficult problem—which can constitute a fundamental level of resistance against them—of guaranteeing the mass production of what I have called "illiterate" specialists and degree-holders: people intelligent and competent in their own domain but completely passive, lacking even the weakest impulse toward comprehension. In all other areas of their lives, they are pure consumers and thus should be ideal functionaries.

Another correction in the picture I have sketched can be located precisely at the level of private life—what Henri Lefebvre called everyday life. The problem of the synthesis between individual private life and public life, between bourgeois and citizen, has been one of the most important in the whole history of European culture. And, following liberal capitalism, cultural creation has most often taken place on one or the other of these planes without synthesizing them. In certain social strata which would have to be studied specifically, the rising standard of living which increases free time and tends to dissipate civic consciousness may give rise to strengthened tendencies toward organizing private life and giving it a meaning. These tendencies could be the point of departure for an active resistance to technocratic society, provided of course that they someday overcome this private level and arrive at an overall problematic.

To put it briefly, even in the liberal era Marx had analyzed reification and the degree of diminution of individual activity which it involved. A situation occurred in which one of the great Western forms of cultural creation had an essentially critical, oppositional nature. Georg Lukács has shown that the structure of the classical novel (a degraded quest for values not conscious in an entirely degraded society, terminating in the hero's awareness of failure) implied a critique of individualistic society in the name of the very values of individual development which the society explicitly extolled but actually made unrealizable. There was at least one common value between classical philosophy and this type of novel: individualism and the development of personal character. But the development of monopoly and then of organizational capitalism, extending reification and hence the passivization of individuals to a degree unknown in liberal society, has suppressed precisely this single common basis. As I have tried to show elsewhere, in certain writings of Robbe-Grillet, Nathalie Sarraute, and Claude Ollier, the New Novel still ascertains the essence of reality but regards society externally, no longer entering into conflict or discussion with it for lack of the common basis which would permit it to do so.

Of course, all the factors and phenomena I have enumerated are complementary and mutually reinforcing. But is it necessary to draw a radically pessimistic conclusion like that of the Frankfurt School sociologists, conceding that all is lost for the humanist tradition and for cultural development? I do not believe so. Every situation created by men has a dialectical character and involves contradictory aspects. Even if the picture I have outlined constitutes the fundamental reality in which the problematic of cultural creation and action unfolds in contemporary industrial societies, the simplistic, apologetic schema sketched at the beginning of this paper nonetheless also includes incontestably real elements. It is true that people in Western societies have a higher standard of living than before, that they have more leisure time, and that mass media have considerably multiplied the possibilities of transmitting to them a mass of information which constitutes, despite everything, genuine elements of a culture. It is also true that this situation includes enhanced possibilities for action, although on the other hand I have mentioned that the resistance to the efficacy of action is augmented and becomes more powerful.

Thus the central problem becomes that of a strategy which would permit efficacious action by those trying to use mass media toward effectively creative, cultural ends. Quite clearly this is a complex problem which involves many questions of detail. I have already mentioned the two contradictions which, among others, can form points of impact for action aiming to produce a formation of consciousness: economic democracy and the problems of everyday life.

I will conclude with a general remark which seems to me the indispensable foundation of any serious attempt to formulate the other problems. Today, at least for those actively participating in production, the main locus of the internal violence and aggression by which the dominant strata perpetuate their domination has changed position. In Western industrial societies this locus is situated less and less on the plane of poverty (which, however, continues to exist for groups which technical progress either eliminates or does not incorporate), or on the plane of terror and physical violence (which, however, are still employed in relations with underdeveloped countries whenever it seems necessary or useful for maintaining relations of domination). Essentially, this locus is on the plane of intellectual violence and the reduction of activity in the field of consciousness. It goes without saying that the reduction of the field of consciousness and the diminution of its activity, far from remaining circumscribed in their own domain, have subsequent repercussions on the ensemble of human life. They tend to prevent individuals from taking an interest in problems of economic, social, and political organization and to lead them increasingly or even exclusively toward engagement in problems of consumption or, at most, in questions of social status and prestige. Inversely, all progress in technocratic society intensifies the reduction of the field of consciousness and the diminution of its activity.

Centered on psychic and individual life, the violence and oppression of the dominant strata have a global, circular character. Breached at any particular point, the gap is immediately closed by pressure exerted in the circle's other sectors. To have the least chance of success, every action defending man and culture must present the same circular, global character.

Every attempt at cultural and solely cultural action necessarily collides with the psychic structure created and developed by organizational capitalism: the passivity, lack of interest, and depoliticization of a large portion of society's members. Likewise, political and social actions oriented toward socialism, economic democracy, and self-management clash with structures of consciousness which make their appeal and message difficult to assimilate.

Thus I think it has become impossible to act in a partial or isolated way, on a single one of these planes. Those who still want to defend the humanist tradition, as well as the development of personal character and of the real intellectual level, must recognize that today the different aspects of the human problematic are more inseparable than ever before. Thus they can gain nothing by acting in their own domain alone, because their action will be ineffective if it is not integrated into an overall struggle. Yet action in any particular domain cannot be considered negligible or secondary in relation to the rest of social life.

More than ever before, cultural action is condemned to sterility if it parts company with economic, social, and political action. But it is also truer than ever before that social, economic, or political action cannot end up outside or ahead of the struggle for consciousness and its activation, which is inseparable from the vitality of cultural life.

3. THE REVOLT OF ARTS AND LETTERS
IN ADVANCED CIVILIZATIONS*

I am still far from able to present an adequate synthesis of the "Revolt in the Literature of Advanced Industrial Societies." But the subjects, writers, and filmmakers I work with nonetheless pose precisely the problem of revolt against contemporary society. Thus I hope to address the fundamental problems by discussing only some concrete examples, which I will try to situate in the very general framework of the problematic of democracy and freedom in advanced industrial societies. It is better to analyze some texts or a writer's work in more or less depth than to conduct the sort of general survey in which only a few words are said about any particular work. Thus, I will first outline the sociological framework for reflection on contemporary cultural life and art.

If we deal with advanced industrial societies then clearly, at least in the West, we are dealing with a universe which sociology, economics, and even history still call the capitalist world (although at present this practice is changing somewhat). But that exact term is beginning to lose its precision, since capitalist society has endured a long time and has passed through different periods. Increased precision thus requires that distinctions be made in the form of a periodization. This must be done not only on the social and economic planes but also on the cultural, philosophical, literary, and

*Written in 1968, this essay was first published in *Liberté et organisation dans le monde actuel* (Brussels, Desclées de Brouwer, Collection du Centre d'Etude de la Civilisation Contemporaine, 1969).

artistic planes, which are intimately linked to the former. Cultural life is not separate from economic, social, and political realities; any periodization (which is indispensable for comprehending the history of capitalism) must be if not identified with, then at least related to, a complementary periodization of philosophical and cultural history. Thus I propose a periodization at the economic level, merely indicating what corresponds to it in philosophy and literature.

There are three distinct periods in the history of Western capitalism, the first of which, extending until about the 1910s, can be called "liberal capitalism." This is the individualist period in which the idea of the ensemble as totality [*l'idée d'ensemble de totalité*] tends to disappear from consciousness. On the plane of thought, this period was expressed above all by two forms of radical individualist philosophy, the two great currents of what we call classical philosophy: rationalism and empiricism. On the literary plane it was expressed by, among other things, the classical novel: the novel of the problematic character.

For sociologists a problem arises even at this level; I will only point it out in passing. On the whole, in the history of Western culture we almost always find a relation of rather strict homology between great philosophical currents and great literary creations;[1] and it is fairly easy to turn up homologous couples in the imaginary universes created by writers and in the conceptual systems elaborated by philosophers.

I merely point out in passing, for example, the couples formed by the works of Pascal and Racine, Descartes and Corneille, Gassendi and Molière, Kant and Schiller, Schelling and the Romantics. But in regard to Enlightenment philosophy, which despite everything is one of the liberal period's most important forms of philosophical thought, no writer can be found who rigorously corresponds to the rationalist current. There is of course the Descartes-Corneille example above; but it is rather unlike the other couples. Descartes' role and his influence in the history of Western culture are enormous, and extend beyond Enlightenment philosophy to contemporary rationalism; whereas only some of Corneille's plays, and not even his entire opus, are the only literary expression relatively akin to the Cartesian position. The disproportion seems obvious between the importance of rationalism in Western culture (especially in the history of Western philosophy) on the one hand, and the importance of Corneille's plays in the history of literature on

---

1. It would of course be necessary to try to verify at the level of positive science whether this parallelism, this homology, can also be extended to the history of painting and the other plastic arts.

the other.

The novel of the problematic character is the literary genre which, because of its importance, corresponds to the era of liberal capitalism. But this novel is not homologous to empiricism, to rationalism, or to Enlightenment philosophy. It is a critical literary form implying a positive element: the affirmation of the individual and of individual value implicit in the novels of this period, from *Don Quixote* to *The Red and the Black* to *Madame Bovary*. But, precisely in this primary affirmation of the individual's value, the novel is an extermely vigorous social critique. It shows that the society in which its heroes live, founded exclusively on the values of individualism and the development of personal character, does not permit the individual to develop or realize himself (I mention this problem only in passing, but obviously it is intimately linked to the problematic of critique and revolt in modern literature).

The second large period in the history of Western capitalism is that currently called the *imperialist* period. I have designated it the period of *capitalism in crisis*, which may indicate its link with literature. The Marxist thinkers who lived and wrote in that era believed a final crisis of capitalism was at hand, the great crisis which would lead to the fall of that order and to the transition to socialism. Today we know that it was actually a period of very acute economic and social crisis, but a period of transition nonetheless. I cannot analyze it in detail, and will point out only the frequency of social and economic crises it evidences, especially as compared with the preceding period.

Historians of imperialism locate the transition from liberal capitalism to this second phase around 1910-1911. Beginning from this date we find WWI in 1914, a profound social and political crisis at the end of the war from 1917-1918, between 1929-1933 an economic crisis of proportions unprecedented in Western history, Hitler's seizure of power in 1933, and WWII between 1939 and 1945 (not to mention the events along the periphery of the advanced industrial world, in Spain and Italy). Evidently, during this entire period economic and social equilibrium was particularly difficult to establish, was realized only provisionally and very unstably, and was followed immediately by the outbreak of new crises.

From the economic viewpoint the explanation is primarily that the mechanism of regulation through the market, essential to the liberal economy, had been disrupted by the development of monopolies and trusts, while the new mechanisms of regulation which characterize the third period had not yet been established.

In any case, on the philosophical plane a specific, original philosophy corresponds to this period of capitalism in crisis. In some respects it conserved individualistic elements (Heidegger's *"Dasein,"* Sartre's *"pour-soi"* in *Being and Nothingness* and the organic subject in *The Critique of Dialectical Reason*); but such elements were centered no longer on reason or perception—on the individual's possibilities—but instead on his limits, and on the limit *par excellence*: death. On the psychic plane this philosophy, existentialism, also gave a central position to the sensibility which developed out of the consciousness of limits and of death: anguish.

With Kafka, Musil, Sartre's *Nausea* and Camus' *The Stranger*, there is in this period a novelistic literature which is much closer to philosophy, and especially to existentialist philosophy. This fact is easily explained insofar as this philosophy explicitly asserted the individual's difficulty in adapting to the surrounding world, a problem already at the center of the novel in the preceding period. It can also be mentioned in passing that from this time, the novel collided with one of the most important of the problems which were to determine its subsequent evolution: the problem of the character. On the economic plane, the transition from liberal capitalism to the capitalism of monopolies and trusts had already been characterized by the individual's loss of economic and social importance. The writer can give form only to what is essential in the reality out of which he elaborates his work. With the individual's importance diminished by economic development, it would have been difficult to create a great literary work relating the story of a character—a biography which, on the plane of reality, had become merely anecdotal.

With the importance socialist thought had gained in the West, there were attempts to replace the character with the collectivity, and to write novels with collective characters (Martin du Gard's *The Thibaults*, for example; the other family novels, Mann's *Buddenbrooks* and Galsworthy's *The Forsyte Saga*; and the novel of the revolutionary community, Malraux's *Man's Fate* [*La Condition humaine*]). But ultimately this was a transitional phase: the socialist revolution did not really transform Western society, the collectivity was not a force capable of changing it, nor did the novel of the collectivity become a predominant literary form.

Finally, the third stage, of special interest to us, is the one in which we live today. Sociologists use various terms to denote this period of capitalism: consumer society, mass society, organizational capitalism, technocratic society. Bascially, each of these designations stresses a principal aspect of a society which, however, constitutes an overall structure. It is initially characterized by the appearance of conscious mechanisms of self-regulation (the market was a mechanism which did not penetrate consciousness, and the period of capitalism in crisis was marked precisely by the lack of effective mechanisms for regulating the economy and the society).

In the liberal period, men's everyday thought, like economics, sociology, and classical philosophy, had completely lost sight of the totality, the ensemble of social life (the overall history of society, production as a whole, etc.). They no longer saw anything but the individual: *homo economicus* in economics; the Cartesian *ego* in philosophy; the autonomy of individual consciousness, reason, and perception; and, in literature, the novel hero. On the contrary, in organizational capitalism the awareness of totality appears to be the fundamental phenomenon, at least on the level of the will and behavior of managers and directors.

Hardly twenty years ago I proposed a thesis on Quesnay's *Le Tableau économique* to a famous professor at the Paris Faculty of Law. He looked at me curiously and said, "That subject is of no interest; it was just an amusement of the Physiocrats." Today one cannot enter a room where a course on political economy is being given without hearing about national accounts, the model of growth, etc.: in other words, about the overall structure of production which was precisely the subject of *Le Tableau économique* and was first studied by the Physiocrats.

To summarize: Marxist thinkers believed capitalism could never integrate a vision of the ensemble of society and of production. But capitalism has survived crises which, according to the Marxists, had to be fatal to it; and its theoreticians have become aware of the problems of the overall organization of society and the economy.

Comparing capitalism in the crisis period between 1910-1912 and 1945 with the preceding period, we find that between 1848 and 1912 there were essentially no important European crises, whereas between 1912 and the end of WWII they followed each other at very short intervals. On the other hand, since the end of that war there have been no more internal crises in Western societies. Of course there were the Algerian events, for example; but they were repercussions on an advanced industrial society from its break with developing countries and with old colonies. Such events are entirely unlike the internal crises of the intermediate era.

These transformations are extremely important and have had considerable consequences. The conscious self-regulation mechanisms developed since the end of WWII have ended up reinforcing a tendency which existed even earlier, but which sociologists had hardly noticed: the integration of the whole society through a rise in the standard of living which, although slow at first, is much greater today (and, in the United States, considerable).

The traditional Marxist schema of the pauperization of the middle classes has lost its validity in Western industrial societies. Of course to a great extent it still applies to developing countries, where differences in the standard of living are extremely marked and poverty is even increasing. But in the industrial societies, in Western capitalism, not only do self-regulation mechanisms lead to a much more rapid rise in the standard of living for the majority of the population; also, one of the psychological consequences of this fact is constituted by the integration of society and the considerable weakening of traditional oppositional forces. This last process is especially important, and it is what those who speak of the affluent society or the consumer society have in mind.

A third and final phenomenon is at once the result of and the precondition for these transformations: the considerable concentration of decision-making power in the hands of a relatively small group (several thousand people) which I will call *technocrats*.[2] For the functioning of their mechanisms, however, advanced industrial societies need an increasing number of professionals with a very high level of knowledge in their specialties. These specialists, whose competence is increasing, who must be highly skilled in their own domains in order to be able to execute the decisions made elsewhere, can be called *technicians*. It must never be forgotten that the greatest part of the lives of these technicians takes place only at the level of execution, the power of decision being reserved to the members of that relatively narrow social stratum which I have called the technocrats.

In these societies where the competence of the social body's members rises considerably, the problem of extreme concentration of decision-making power becomes fundamental: the rise in competence does not lead the great majority of individuals to participate in essential decisions. This fact has extremely serious psychic consequences. Here I will not analyze it psychologically or sociologically in depth; but clearly the most important result of this phenomenon is the considerable reduction of the psychic life of individuals.

---

2. To avoid any misunderstanding it should be stressed that the term "technocrat" used in this sense by no means signifies a superior technical cadre specifically concerned with the production process, but denotes a member of that stratum which participates in the important, basic decisions concerning the life of society. Thus there are technocrats of education, politics, the economy, cultural life, etc., in addition, of course, to technocrats of production.

It is not true that the rising level of knowledge and professional skill necessarily and implicitly entails expanded freedom, intensified psychic and intellectual life, or strengthened possibilities of comprehension. What I once called "the illiterate specialist" is a danger which threatens to grow considerably in organizational society. Herbert Marcuse has posed this question strikingly in *One-Dimensional Man*, although in my judgment his conclusions are too pessimistic.

Traditionally, during the entire history preceding our contemporary societies (and probably also in the present and the future, although there things are not as clear), man has defined himself in terms of two fundamental dimensions in which his psychic life and his behavior develop: the tendency to adapt to the real, and the tendency to overcome the real toward the possible—toward a beyond which men must create by their behavior.

Adaptation to the real is an essential function for the individual as much as for social groups. Such adaptation, however, tends to create equilibria which threaten to become static. Until now society always changed due not only to the action of the individuals and groups composing it but also to external influences. Thus, well before it was attained (usually as it was only being approached), equilibration was no longer adapted to the real problems of social life; and men came to be oriented toward a different and often higher equilibrium.

Although I cannot pursue the point—I have written a book on the subject[3]—I will say that the *possible* is the fundamental category for comprehending human history. The great difference between positivist and dialectical sociology consists precisely in the fact that whereas the former is content to develop the most exact and meticulous possible photography of the existing society, the latter tries to isolate the potential consciousness in the society it studies: the potential [*virtuelles*], developing tendencies oriented toward overcoming that society. In short, the first tries to give an account of the functioning of the existing structuration, and the second centers on the possibilities of varying and transforming social consciousness and reality.

Pascal grasped this phenomenon early, saying that man cannot be defined without self-contradiction because the only valid definition of man is that he is infinitely more than what he is. In a dialectical perspective which is not Pascal's, I would add that man is greater than what he is because he is always making himself and making a

---

3. *The Human Sciences and Philosophy*, tr. Hayden V. White and Robert Anchor (London, Jonathan Cape, 1969).

new world.

But the fundamental problematic of modern capitalist societies is no longer located at the level of poverty—although, I repeat, poverty remains even in the most advanced industrial countries—or even at the level of a freedom directly limited by law or external constraint. Instead, it lies entirely in the contraction of the level of consciousness and in the concomitant tendency to reduce the fundamental human dimension of the possible. As Marcuse says, if social evolution does not change direction, man will live and act increasingly only in the single dimension of adaptation to reality, and not in the other, the dimension of transcendence.

The contraction of personal character and individuality is a disquieting phenomenon even in the transitional period in which we are living. It threatens to become increasingly serious if social evolution is actually oriented toward men's perfect adaptation to a society where most of them become mere well-paid functionaries with a high standard of living and long vacations, living better and better—but with a restricted consciousness—as specialized technicians. This, I believe, is the fundamental problem of technocratic society.

Nonetheless, in opposition to Marcuse I believe there are tendencies toward overcoming this situation. One-dimensional man (to use the singularly well-chosen formulation he originated) represents only one of the alternatives. facing contemporary industrial societies. Here I will not enter into this large problem, but will restrict myself to analyzing the types of reactions produced out of this situation at the level of literary and cultural creation, and especially the revolt within that creation.

This revolt can be comprised and described under two different, complementary aspects. There is the formal revolt of an art which, not accepting a society, refuses it by finding new forms of expression unlike those which that society has created and in which it has traditionally seen itself. I believe it necessary to comprehend the first manifestations of the New Novel, and a whole series of today's literary works, on the basis of this extremely important phenomenon. The other aspect is the theme of revolt itself in the work of certain writers and artists.

Despite the intimate link uniting these two aspects of negation, there is nonetheless a fundamental difference between them. In one case it is a matter of refusing society, a revolt expressed through the invention of new forms; in the other, the problem of men's revolt in and against the society they refuse is treated in the work itself and forms its subject, theme, central concern, and structuration. I will deal very quickly with the first of these two aspects of revolt in order to move on to a brief analysis of the work of the greatest writer of the revolt in French literature today, Jean Genet, in his theater from *The Maids* to *The Screens*.

It goes without saying that I begin with the idea that a great writer cannot write a valid work at any time or in any place. In the first place, he can write only in an overall perspective which he has not invented and which must exist in society so that he can subsequently transpose it in a coherent imaginary universe. Secondly, this imaginary universe will constitute a valid work only insofar as it centers on the essential aspects of the social reality which has helped to elaborate the categories structuring it. I will not dwell on this undeniably difficult business; I will merely say that this is the translation of a central idea of Hegelian philosophy, the identity of subject and object, into the language of the sociology of culture.

But in contemporary society the important phenomenon is the loss and progressive disappearance of the individual's importance and of the meaning of what is immediately lived on one hand, and the tendency to constrict consciousness on the other. Writers' resistance to this rising and developing society thus encounters a double obstacle. On the one hand it is in fact no longer possible to address the great problems of modern society, of man in today's world, at the level of an immediately perceived story. The biography of a character has become merely anecdotal. Narration restricted to things and events at the immediately lived level risks remaining in miscellaneous fact with no essential meaning. Inversely, if the writer tries to address the overall problems he must place himself at a level which, although not conceptual (no great work of art is conceptual), nonetheless becomes totalizing and increasingly loses relation with the perceived and the immediately lived. And this occurs at a time when, because of the psychic and intellectual constriction I have described, the consciousness of the individuals living in society (of the great majority of readers) becomes less and less suited to grasping phenomena at this level of abstraction and generality. Two examples will clarify these observations.

One of the best-known studies of Robbe-Grillet has been published by an American professor.[4] In this extremely intelligent, penetrating study he has demonstrated that each of this author's narratives contains a narrated story which, with some ability to follow the text very closely, can be extracted; and that in certain

---

4. Bruce Morrissette, *Les Romans de Robbe-Grillet* (Paris: Editions de Minuit, 1963, 1965, 1971).

respects this story ultimately resembles those narrated in the novels of the liberal capitalist era. From this he concludes that Robbe-Grillet's originality lies primarily in the fact that his way of narrating the story is different from that of earlier writers.

In the course of a long discussion with this critic I tried to maintain that if a writer narrates things differently it is because things themselves have become essentially different, and therefore he can no longer say them in the accepted way. The discussion ended with the analysis of a passage from *Jealousy*: "The light, rubber-soled shoes make no sound on the hallway tiles."[5] The critic says, "Clearly, this involves a jealous man who walks very softly so as not to make noise and surprise his wife." I replied, "Perhaps what is essential is simply that Robbe-Grillet wrote not 'a man walks very softly' but instead 'the light...shoes...make no sound,' probably because what was essential was the fact that in today's world the shoes carry the man: the motor of events is no longer man but inert objects."

The reply, of course, was, "This is no doubt an amusing, ingenious witticism, but nevertheless a witticism." Then I asked my interlocutor to choose between two statements which I would present and tell me which he found more accurate, understanding that the answer to the problem at issue would depend on this choice. One could say that every year between July and August some millions of people in advanced industrial countries take vacations, carrying cameras and taking photographs which they then show to their friends and family. Or one could say that every year, in rarely explicit, usually implicit accord with certain travel agencies, the boards of directors of Kodak and the major camera firms decide to produce a certain number of cameras which will travel around the world, while a certain number of other cameras sold in previous years will remain in circulation. These decisions once made, the cameras set out on their travels with a corresponding number of people to operate them. Which of these formulations gives the best account of the phenomenon's essential reality?

Any serious sociologist, I think, will choose the second. And insofar as it permits the more exact comprehension of reality it is also chosen in the literary transposition which leads Robbe-Grillet to say "the soles move forward" rather than "the man moves forward." But this is a fundamental change and the writer can express it only at this level of abstraction, which makes him seem paradoxical to

---

5. *Jealousy*, in *Two Novels by Robbe-Grillet*, tr. Richard Howard (New York: Grove Press, Inc., 1965) p. 58.

most people who read his text. Men live at the level of immediate perceptions and thus, confronted with a text of this sort, they say, "This is absurd," and return to the immediately grasped and lived viewpoint which remains superficial and does not touch the essence of the phenomenon. But consciously or unconsciously, the great writer tries precisely to reach this essence and to say what is essential. The story of a jealous man is only a miscellaneous fact whereas, whether or not we are conscious of it, the soles which carry the man have on the whole become the central phenomenon of our everyday life.

Another example: I made a test by asking a certain number of people who had seen Godard's film *Contempt* to tell me its subject. So far, the responses have been almost unfailingly of the same type: "A couple falls apart because the woman begins to scorn the man." Just once, I believe, someone answered, "It's about a book; the *Odyssey*, I think." But the film's apparent subject is the impossibility of being loved in a world where one cannot film the *Odyssey*. It can now be comprehended in only two ways: the dying, cultivated, traditional humanism of Fritz Lang, who knows that the gods appear in the *Odyssey* and have disappeared from the world in which he finds himself; or Prokosch's view, which does not even recognize that there were gods in the *Odyssey*. Although the problem of the *Odyssey* and its cinematic transposition is present almost constantly in the film, most spectators have not even noticed it.

Godard's film attempts to circumscribe the Lang-Prokosch opposition. Becoming aware of the problem, the woman comes to scorn her husband, who understands nothing of the world around him and lives in total unconsciousness. Love is impossible in a world where there are no more gods, where adapted men do not even know what "god" or "love" might mean or what meaning those words might give their existence. The film ends with collision and death between two stationary vehicles, symbolically prolonging the opposition between Lang and Prokosch as the former continues to film a caricatural *Odyssey* in front of a hopelessly empty sea.

Although the *Odyssey* is in the background, Godard gives the problems of film, the discussions of the *Odyssey*, and the Lang-Prokosch opposition materially greater room than he gives the rest of the story. But if you try the experiment you will see the extent to which spectators have not even perceived this essential aspect of the film.

This is the central problem for literary creation today. The writer wants to express the problematic of the gods' absence in the modern world (the gods signify fundamental values and the possibilities of individual realization). But access to this problematic is difficult or impossible for most of his readers; they are hardly aware that the soles are really what move the man forward and carry him... Taking a whole series of important modern books and films, one can find the same problematic, which film-makers and writers cannot address on the immediate level of Pierre's or Jean's life story because that has become a mere anecdote. A film like *Contempt* addresses it at the level of a couple's story. But to do so, it must overcome that story and thus become incomprehensible in a society where reading is increasingly oriented toward professional problems and immediate life, and where the very possibility of comprehending the problematic of the gods' existence (what Marcuse called man's dimension of the possible) is considerably reduced. This situation gives rise to a difficult art which no longer seems to speak immediately to the reader, although every great writer—and there are still several of them—does everything he can to make himself understood (I am speaking not of epigones but of truly creative works). For this reason, criticism today is assuming an increasingly important role.

I have mentioned only two examples, *Jealousy* and *Contempt*, but I could reconsider the problem by analyzing about twenty literary works and films. Almost all contemporary art is an art of refusal which inquires into man's existence in the modern world and which, in order to do so, must take place on an abstract level. It can no longer speak with the aid of the story of an individual or even an account of a lived event, because the individual himself is no longer an essential element of contemporary society as he was in the age of Stendhal, Balzac, and Flaubert. Thus results what I call the revolt on the formal plane, which is necessary in order to remain at the level of essentials and of authentic creation. An art which refuses this society, a humanist art signalling the dangers it presents for man, must necessarily speak this new language.

This leads to the problem of the public's comprehension of contemporary literature and art. Godard's films enjoy a relative success; but when you try to ask spectators what the films are saying you discover the extent to which the message fails to come across despite the success. Let me recall another anecdote. One day after a showing of Godard's film *La Chinoise* I was in a cafe, next to respectable people who were discussing the film they had seen. They tried to outdo each other with statements like, "The film is absurd, ridiculous; it doesn't make sense and doesn't mean anything," "It makes fun of us, it takes us for idiots," and so forth. The conversation continued in this vein for about ten minutes until one lady, in a peremptory tone and with the air of making the most negative possible statement about the film, concluded it: "In a word, it's like Picasso."

A single process obliges writers to speak less and less at the level of immediate perception and prevents the public, except in exceptional cases and by special efforts, from understanding them and overcoming the immediately perceived. In such a society, how can this art convey its meaning? That is the problem.

The other side of the problematic is oppositional thought and the theme of revolt in literature. So far, industrial societies seem solidly integrated at the level of their external and more or less visible manifestations. In a book written three or four years ago[6] I said that the forces of transformation in contemporary technocratic society may not be as weak as they might seem on the manifest perceptual level. These forces would have to be studied sociologically in depth; but in fact, literature has been written until now in a society where the forces of contestation seem to be growing increasingly weaker. Therefore, exactly as writers can no longer relate the story of an individual in a universe where this individual no longer has any essential reality, neither can they relate the story of forces of contestation which no longer exist or are disappearing. For this reason the literature of revolt has gained only a relatively secondary place in the recent development of contemporary literature.

Nonetheless, a very great writer, Jean Genet, has placed this problem at the center of his work in his last four plays: *The Maids, The Balcony, The Blacks,* and *The Screens.* Moreover, the study of these texts raises a rather important problem of aesthetic sociology which I will only note in passing. In my seminar we are studying existentialism and, although we cannot explain it at this point, we find that at the very moments Genet and Sartre tackled the themes of class struggle, revolt, and revolution, they both moved from prose and the novel to the theater.

The great existentialist works of the first period are clearly *The Wall* and *Nausea*, but in them Sartre does not address the problem of history and revolution at all. When he did engage that problematic he still tried to write a novel, *The Roads to Freedom*, which had enormous success at the time. But whereas *The Wall* and *Nausea* are still read today, to most serious critics *The Roads to Freedom* appears to be a failed novel (and Sartre himself never finished it). He will subsequently address the new problematic in a series of plays, from *The Flies* to *The Condemned of Altona*. To a

6. *Pour une sociologie du roman* (Paris: Gallimard, 1964).

great extent the problems of revolution form the theme of these plays; but the author still addresses them in the perspective of classical philosophy: the relation between the individual and external social reality (Orestes and revolution, Goetz and history, Frantz and torture). In short, as opposed to the theme of his novels the question in almost all of Sartre's plays is the conflict between the ethical and the historical.

Almost exactly the same thing occurred in Genet's work. He begins as a novelist. He writes a play, *Deathwatch*, which is rather average since it is still centered on the old problematic. Then the conflict between dominated and dominators appears in his work, and he writes his four great plays. This judgment does not express a merely personal opinion; objectively, it suffices to ascertain the frequencies of performance: *Deathwatch* is rarely performed whereas *The Maids, The Balcony, The Blacks,* and *The Screens* play throughout the world. Above all, the public perceives Genet's plays as "poetic": if that means anything, it usually means simply, "They are very beautiful; I like them, but I don't know why." But these are complex plays whose structure is not grasped at first and which, in analysis, appear extremely rigorous, to the point that there is a reason for almost every phrase being exactly where it is. These four plays also have a common basic structure, which I will now try to outline.

A first common element distinguishes them from all the rest of contemporary literature: the characters are collective. There are no individual characters except, to some extent, Said in *The Screens*; but he is defined in relation to collective forces and, in addition, is not entirely individual in that he is part of the group formed by himself, his mother, and his wife Leila. In *The Maids* there are Monsieur and Madame on the one hand, Solange and Claire on the other; in *The Balcony* there are the characters of the balcony on the one hand, and on the other the rebels and the populace who come to the house of illusions; in *The Blacks* there are the Blacks and the Whites; in *The Screens* there are the colonists, the rebels, and the dead, not to mention the army and the prostitutes.

Clearly, insofar as historical action forms the theme and problematic of a work, the forces acting are not individuals but groups, since individual time is only biographical whereas historical time is that of groups. But after Malraux, whose literary work already dates from a number of years ago, Genet has been the only important writer of contemporary literature who has presented the conflict of collective forces.

What are the relations between these collective characters? At least for the first three of these plays and to some extent for the fourth, the subject is the opposition, the conflict between dominated and dominators, with the dominated assuming a different face each time (the Maids, the Blacks, the populace and the rebels in *The Balcony*, and the colonized people; to whom are opposed Monsieur and Madame, the Whites, the powers of the Balcony, the colonists or the victorious group of colonial rebels in *The Screens*).

Conflict in these four plays also presents certain common traits. In the first place, the dominated people's feelings toward their dominators are complex, comprising two contradictory elements: hate and fascination. Hate and fascination are justified in the plays and create the coherence of their universe because all attempts by the dominated to destroy the dominators end in failure. The Maids want to kill Madame but cannot succeed; in *The Balcony* the rebels cannot destroy the established order (this problem will be seen to be posed somewhat differently in *The Blacks* and especially in *The Screens*). This failure justifies the fascination of the dominated with the dominators' power.

The dominated can realize only ritual in this universe. Ritual comprises two elements which, although they do not always have the same proportions or weight in each play, are nonetheless present in each. In *The Maids, The Balcony,* and *The Blacks*, the dominated play at destroying—killing—the dominators, and as well at being the dominators. In this ritual, hate inspires the destructive aspect, fascination the identification. The Maids play at being Madame and at killing Madame. In *The Balcony* the populace play at being the powerful and at destroying them by revolution. We find the same situation in *The Blacks* and also, partially, in *The Screens*.

A final element of this universe: the real is always deceptive, inauthentic, and even odious; whereas on the contrary the only authentic, profound values are unquestionably those of the ritual. Nothing is true but appearance; nothing is human but the imaginary, even if it never succeeds in transforming reality.

In their reception, however, these plays have encountered a fundamental misunderstanding on this point. Certain critics (especially the particularly intelligent American critic Lionel Abel, but also many others) have presented Genet as the poet of appearance. Abel, moreover, has drawn all the consequences of this analysis, remarking that Genet, a very great writer in the beginnings of his plays, becomes much weaker in his endings. In fact, such a view cannot see why the plays do not end in the perspective in which they begin; why the Maids finally commit suicide or why Roger mutilates or kills himself at the end of *The Balcony*. If the appearance is marvellous and the imaginary alone is valid, the characters would have to delight in that; one cannot see what leads them to despair. Faced with this discrepancy the critics—instead of asking "Isn't Genet saying something else? Haven't I made a mistake?"—stick by their interpretation at the risk of failing to understand the work in its entirety. Even if ritual is the only valid thing in this universe, it is not satisfactory. Each play leads to the problematic of passage from the imaginary to the real; the impossibility of this passage creates despair: the Maids' suicide, Roger's self-mutilation, and, in a more complex way which will be discussed shortly, the ending of *The Screens.*

This, then, is the universe of the four plays. I will now try to address their differences, starting with the first two.

Genet did everything he could to make *The Maids* clear. A passage which seems to me absolutely central is the one where the Maids and Madame say the same things (that they love Monsieur and will follow him even to the penal colony). But when the Maids say this it is authentic, dramatic, and human; whereas coming from Madame it becomes ridiculous and odious. In fact, every evening the Maids play at being Madame and killing Madame; every evening they resume a ritual in which Claire plays at being Madame and Solange at being Claire. They have tried to kill Madame in reality as in the ritual, but have never succeeded. In addition, they have testified falsely against Monsieur, who has been imprisoned.

When the curtain rises we witness one of these soirées. Imagining they are Madame, Claire and Solange tell us how much they love Monsieur with an authentic love—Monsieur who may be convicted. At this point Madame arrives. With only some slight stylistic variations, she says the same thing, and it becomes absolutely odious. It is odious because, in the first place, Madame speaks in the conditional: she explains that Monsieur will make an agreement and will never be deported but that, if he were deported, she would follow him even to the penal colony. It is odious because, although she has declared that nothing interests her any longer, that she is going to give away her furs, and that she no longer wants to check the accounts, learning that Monsieur will be freed is enough to make her ask for the accounts and reclaim her furs: we understand that she had never stopped thinking about them. Finally, it is odious when in the final phrase of her great tirade she exclaims, "Solange, give me a cigarette."

Thus from beginning to end the play centers on the authenticity of the imaginary as opposed to the sordidness of real life; on the human and dramatic—although humbled—Maids as opposed to the deceitful and ridiculous Madame. But Monsieur is freed. It becomes clear that the Maids will be arrested for false testimony, will not be able to continue their daily ritual, and will have to acknowledge defeat. They try anew to poison Madame but, as the text says, objects themselves conspire in her favor: Madame cannot be destroyed, she is too strong. To triumph in the imaginary the Maids can only destroy themselves. At the end, Madame is magnanimous as always. Believing the Maids adore her, she will pity the poor Claire killed by the evil Solange; but Solange will respond, "I am no longer the maid: I am Mademoiselle Solange." The play ends with an evocation of Holy Communion which is not at all parodic: Claire drinks the poison from a precious vessel, in accord with Solange.[7]

We find the same schema in the next play, *The Balcony*, whose action is otherwise the literary transposition of the great transformations of contemporary Western society. In the Balcony are the powerful, the Chief of Police and the proprietress, Madame Irma; below is the populace which comes to the house of illusions to play at being powerful. In fact, they play at being what everyone imagines to be powerful—at being general, bishop, or judge— whereas society was transformed long ago, and the truly powerful are the Chief of Police and Madame Irma, the proprietress of the house of illusions. The play's subject is the series of events (at the level of a poetic transposition) which has made society conscious of these transformations, and which creates the situation at the end of the play in which people come to the house of illusions no longer to play judge or general, but to play chief of police. As related in the play, this evolution corresponds rigorously to the history of Western society, in which awareness has resulted to a very great extent from the revolutionary threat during the post-WWI years and from the defeat of the forces favorable to revolution.[8]

The way of formulating the problem of ritual here is homologous to that in *The Maids*: identification and desire for destruction in the imaginary. I will restrict myself to the first three scenes in the house of illusions. The first tells us precisely that the real bishop cannot be a true bishop: he cannot realize the essence of a bishop because it is incompatible with reality. A real bishop is obliged to accept

7. For a more detailed analysis of these four plays see Lucien Goldmann, "La théâtre de Genet. Essai d'étude sociologique" in *Structures mentales et création culturelle* (Paris: Editions Anthropos, 1970).

8. From the side of Eastern society, moreover, there is a homological transposition in Witold Gombrowicz's play *The Marriage*, which shows how technocratic society and the predominance of the executive arose out of revolutionary victory.

innumerable compromises and deceptions; whereas the essence of the bishop, who must refuse every compromise, can be found only in the imaginary: in the house of illusions. The second scene tells us that the imaginary judge, who realizes the essence of the judge, depends on the criminal's existence and essence. Finally the third of these scenes, involving the general, shows us the extent to which imaginary essence constitutes the only poetic and authentic value. Of course these three aspects coexist in the three scenes, but with a different accent in each.

Then there is the revolt, during which the populace gains awareness of the power held by the Chief of Police and the proprietress of the house of illusions, Madame Irma. The real bishop, judge, and general having been killed in the course of the struggle, the powers of the Balcony replace them with the populace in the house of illusions: they are made bishop, judge, and general in reality. Of course, this transformation deprives them of all pathetic, dramatic character, and returns them to the level of mere caricatures.

Roger, the revolutionary leader, understood the importance of organization, demanded it, and opposed whoever defended dream, spontaneity, or authenticity. After the defeat he comes to the house of illusions and asks to play the chief of police. This is the great event which everyone has long awaited. But very soon he explains it himself: he is chief of police only in appearance, whereas he would have liked to be the chief of the executive in reality. As the Maids killed themselves, he will mutilate himself (a way of telling us that he will kill himself). Having thus entered the imagination of the entire society, the chief of police will reign there for two thousand years.

In *The Blacks* we find the same problem. Moreover the powers, the dominators, the Whites in the Balcony are the same characters as in the preceding play: soldier, magistrate, cleric, queen, and servant (who corresponds to the queen's messenger in *The Balcony*). Nothing could better underline the link between the two plays; but the critics have almost never perceived it. Genet has again done everything to be clear; certainly it is not his fault if he has not been understood.

But a new aesthetic problem arises in the analysis of this play. The Whites cannot be played by white actors and the Blacks by blacks. As in the preceding play, the central theme is the radical opposition between dominated and dominators (here, Blacks and Whites); and this theme would be contradicted in the course of a performance involving collaboration between them. Thus the Whites must be played by Blacks who carry white masks, while constantly letting it be seen that they are masks. And at a certain moment Genet has the masks raised in order to make them actors again and to explain their solidarity with those playing the role of the dominated.

The play is constructed on the same schema as the two preceding ones. At the beginning the Blacks perform the periodic ritual of assassinating a white woman, a ritual in which they must be condemned by the Whites at the end. And just as the Maids can only kill themselves, just as Roger ends up mutilating himself, only outside the play's action do the Blacks kill another Black who, the whole play suggests, has betrayed them. At a certain point, however, the action is transformed. Ville de Saint-Nazaire, who establishes the link with the outside, returns to the stage to say that after this execution a new chief will come, who perhaps will lead the Blacks to victory. At this point the ritual's aim seems to change, and the play ends with the imaginary destruction of the Whites. Victory still exists only on the plane of ritual, of the imaginary; but it exists nonetheless, and replaces defeat.

The play's problematic is especially clear in a repeated scene, with which I will stop. The ritual centers on a murder, but the various participants do not want to join in the scheme. Archibald, the game's ringleader, always has to collect them and recall them to the roles they must play. Vertu and Village, a pair of lovers, explain that their love for each other suffices them and that they do not need to participate in the ritual. Archibald's response, which in part provides the key to the play, is substantially this: "You cannot love, because you can do so only with white words. But to be able to use them you have to be not on the stage but in the drawing-room, among the Whites who don't accept you. You are Blacks; and love between Blacks, between the dominated, is impossible in the world of those who dominate you, and impossible with words not your own. First a new world must be created and, corresponding to that world, a new language: then you could really engage in a love that would be yours, a black love." Less clearly expressed, this theme has already been encountered in *The Maids.* Solange and Claire's love for the milkman can only be sordid: the sole authentic love is their love for Monsieur; identifying with Madame, they imagine they will follow him even to the penal colony the day he is convicted. This is why at the end of *The Blacks,* when the play's action is practically finished, the ritual accomplished, and the Whites executed, as the other actors retire from the stage we see Vertu and Village remaining and restating the same problem. Village wants to hug Vertu in his arms:

VERTU: All men are like you: they imitate. Can't you invent something else?

VILLAGE: For you I could invent anything: fruits, brighter words, a two-wheeled wheelbarrow, cherries without pits, a bed for three, a needle that doesn't prick. But gestures of love, that's harder... Still, if you really want me to...

VERTU: I'll help you. At least, there's one thing: you won't be able to wind your fingers in my long golden hair...[9]

This ending accords with the fact that the situation outside it is no longer the same. There is a new black leader, and the ritual enters a struggle which may lead to freedom. Without moving from the defeat of the dominated to their real victory and the defeat of the dominators, the play shows at least the possibility or hope of it. And, on the plane of Vertu and Village's love, this change is also the reason that hope of finding words which would permit their love's realization can appear.

Finally, Genet has written a fourth play, *The Screens*, which is much more complex but begins with a universe whose schema is analogous to the one we are already acquainted with: the opposition of dominated and dominators. But this time the play's subject is the victory of the dominated. In the course of the action three social orders appear: the order of the dominated and the dominators, of colonized and colonists, which we have already encountered; then the order of the victorious rebels; and finally the order of the dead.

As a sociologist I will point out that these three orders correspond to three concepts of the group held by the radical left, whose vision Genet has transposed in his entire theater. There is the society of exploitation constituted by the dominated-dominator opposition; the not yet ideal society in which the victorious dominated take power but maintain the State; and finally the dreamed-of society which abolishes all contradictions and reconciles everyone, where all the contradictons which placed men in opposition during their lives on Earth have disappeared and where, leaving aside all that formerly separated them, old enemies understand each other.

But there is a group opposed to these three orders. This opposition could have been an individual's, Said's; but we have already seen that at his side Said has his wife Leila and his mother. These three characters are not identical, since there is a hierarchization until the

---

9. *The Blacks*, tr. Bernard Frechtman (New York: Grove Press, Inc., 1960) p. 128.

end of the play (Said is much more anarchic and oppositional than Leila or his mother); but they form a group opposing all the orders it encounters in the course of the action.

In addition to this fundamental theme of the relations between the three orders and Said, his wife, and his mother, there are two other parts of this particularly complex play which are transformed in a parallel way in the unfolding of the main action: the brothel and the army.

The story of the brothel, which I will outline very quickly, parallels the transformation and succession of the three orders. Moreover, there are three prostitutes corresponding to the three orders and to the two transformations constituting the passages from one to another. At the outset the brothel is the imaginary universe, the universe of ritual where the colonized come to find authenticity and essence. And as I have already said, as in all four plays, this is the only authenticity which can exist in a world where the colonists, the dominators, are odious or ridiculous and where the colonized find themselves in the same situation as the Maids, the populace, or the Blacks. In the brothel the perfect prostitute, Warda, represents this authentic universe of the imaginary.

In the second episode, the prostitutes themselves say that they have been integrated into the society and the struggle. They now have a function in revolutionary combat. They are respected, saluted, received, and accepted by the others as members of society. Their function, having become real, has replaced the imaginary one; their activity has become part of life. This situation is incarnated in Malika, the prostitute who from the beginning had relations with the resistance.

Finally there is the plane of the third order, of the revolutionaries' victory and, somewhere in the distance, the appearance of the order of the dead. Here we see the society born of the victory of the dominated depriving the brothel of all value. Warda is killed; Malika moves to the second plane; and another prostitute who arrives from the North and no longer has any valid social function will replace them. In fact one of the play's central problems, or perhaps even its central problem, is that the rebels' victory has created a universe which denies both nonconformity and the imaginary: the latter no longer has a place in this new world (and the rebels' view is the same as that of the soldiers who once fought in defense of the dominators). Precisely for this reason, Said cannot accept this world. It can be seen how rigorously homologous, functional, and meaningful these transformations of the brothel are in relation to the succession of the three orders which forms the play's main subject.

Now a word about the army, since this aspect of the play has provoked all the trouble and has been least understood by the public. Here I will address a fundamental problem of literary criticism. A rather questionable practice in criticism consists of relating all the events and problems it encounters in a writer's work to his personality and his deep aspirations.[10] But criticism agrees on this, particularly on the existence of a connection between the homosexuality it finds in Genet's writing and the deep yearnings of his personality, to such an extent that at the Venice Biennial a known critic seriously stated that the Living Theater had had men perform *The Maids*, "as Genet wished." But Genet's preface to the play says explicitly that it must be played by women. For this critic and his audience, it was so obvious that homosexuality is fundamental in Genet's work that they unquestioningly accepted the idea that the women in *The Maids* must be played by men.

Actually, the homosexuality which is constant in the novels and in the first play, *Deathwatch*, disappears in Genet's other plays or can be found there only through highly questionable interpretations. The important loves are all heterosexual: the love of the Maids for Monsieur or the milkman, of Village for Vertu, of Roger for Chantal, of Said for Leila. Homosexuality disappears from this theater, reappearing only in the single relation of the lieutenant and the sergeant in the army of *The Screens*. If it wants to be taken seriously, any scientific attempt to relate homosexuality in Genet's work to his biography or personality must account for this disappearance and reappearance. Why does homosexuality vanish in the passage from the novel to theater? Why does it reappear in this single part of *The Screens*?

Formulating the problem at the level of structural analysis clarifies matters. Nonconformity, the refusal of the existing world, is an essential element in the structure of Genet's work. But in his novels, from *Thief's Journal* to the first play, *Deathwatch*, Genet structures his universe only with values definitively recognized by society. The attempt to extract the elements constituting this universe uncovers an ensemble of mature relations, especially those of love, friendship, and courage. Limited to their relations at the level of their immediate assertion, these elements can provide the material for a very beautiful romantic book, but not at all for a

---

10. I add that, on the contrary, all my work tends to show that the only problems posed by a valid work are aesthetic problems linked with the coherent expression of a world view, which most often have relatively little to do with the author's personality.

nonconformist work. Since the anticonformist element was essential to the meaning and message of the writer's universe, he had only a single possibility of obtaining it: to the structure formed by these elements he had to add a second dimension which renders them nonconformist and is, if you wish, oblique. For this reason Genet added the second aspect to all the constitutive values of his pre-theatrical work, making those values unacceptable to the existing society: love, no doubt, but homosexual love; courage, but courage in crime; friendship, but friendship in vice and in socially condemned behavior; etc.

When Genet joins the radical left, primarily the group around Sartre and *Les Temps Modernes*, discovering the universe of class struggle and transposing it in his work, he no longer needs this second, oblique dimension to make the work nonconformist and to introduce social criticism into it. Also apparent is the abrupt disappearance of everything which was connected with that dimension, especially homosexuality. The question thus involves not a problem of personal expression but an aesthetic problem.

But then why does homosexuality reappear precisely in the army of *The Screens*? There is a very analogous reason, which is not in the least a mere desire to denigrate or caricature. In the first part, the colonists are drawn very caricaturally; otherwise Genet would have to resort to the oblique dimension. In the case of the army, the reason involved seems exactly the reverse, since in *The Screens* the army no longer struggles for victory. This army has already lost the war and no longer does anything but celebrate a ritual, conducting an imaginary war. But in Genet's universe, where reality appears unacceptable, this situation gives the army an essential, positive value.

The problem arose before in *The Blacks*: "Grief, sir, is another of their adornments" says Snow,[11] and Archibald explains that this risk had to be run if the Whites were to be fought. And it was for this reason that some actors in the ritual, especially Snow, did not want to participate in this destruction.

That is to say that Genet again encounters a problem analogous to that of his first works. In fact, by valorizing the army because in the play it is situated in ritual and the imaginary, he risks apologizing for an institution which still really exists in society. In the effort to avoid this misunderstanding, all the old oblique dimensions reappear.

To go to the center of the problem we should analyze the scene

---

11. Genet, *op. cit.*, p. 11.

which, more than any other, has provoked scandal. To consider only what it ways in substance, it can first be analyzed leaving the oblique dimension aside. This army is no longer struggling for victory, its combat has therefore become essential and authentic. It is important to each of its members not to die alone in an alien world, and to preserve the familiar surroundings of its native land to the maximum extent. When the lieutenant dies, all the others sacrifice to give his more trivial death the values which they have conserved in order to guarantee themselves less woeful deaths.

If we remain at this level, where the dying lieutenant's comrades join together to help him and to make his death less solitary, the scene is pathetic and romantic. To avoid this valorization, Genet has added the coarseness which provoked scandal. But it has been said before in *The Blacks*: when the dominators are conquered they become authentic and acceptable. The problematic is clear, as is the reason why we must not stop at the coarseness but must try to comprehend the play's structural ensemble and the problematic which has given rise to this aspect of it, which in fact seems to me aesthetically questionable.

Thus, the main action is framed by two parallel actions: the brothel on one side, the army on the other. This action itself is perfectly coherent and precise. First there is the order of oppression, where authenticity exists only in the imaginary. Then there is the revolt, begun by Said, who rejects it at the very instant when it becomes general (when the others say to him and his mother, "You were right; we join you," he will refuse to join forces with them and will remain isolated to preserve his nonconformity and individual autonomy). Finally there is the victory; and at that moment the problem of Said's status in the new order arises. To those previously dominated who, since the victory, have become dominators, the collective symbolic figure Ommu will explain that, now that they have replaced the old powers,[12] their revolt can be justified only to the extent that it can build a free world where nonconformity is not only possible but has a sanction and a recognized function: a universe with a place for singing and for Said's values. The new masters do not understand this perspective: with the struggle ended, they are at most disposed to pardon Said, accepting him and expunging the past. But Ommu replies that the question is one not of pardoning but of the very nature of the order they are creating,

---

12. They are less ridiculous than the colonists because, perhaps contrary to the play's deep coherence, Genet wants to maintain the difference in value between the old and new orders by not putting both on the same plane.

which cannot be justified so long as it must merely pardon non-conformity. The play ends when one of the new masters fires the gunshot which kills Said.

Despite the appearance of a fortuitous accident which she had wanted to create, The Mother in fact participated in the revolt and the resistance; therefore she has entered the kingdom of the dead. There she awaits Leila and her son. But, less radical than Said, Leila does not accept the order of the dead: she will not enter it, but will nonetheless send her veil. Said, the nonconformist who remains alive until the end, is probably the first positive character in contemporary avant-garde literature; he neither accepts the order of the dead nor will he send any sign or trace there, and instead will pass directly into nothingness. He has remained alive from the beginning to the end of the play. For the first time in the modern universe, the world of freedom is affirmed, through him, as something which can open up a hope for the future.

Genet seems alone among great contemporary authors in having written a play whose axis is primarily the dimension of the possible and of transcendence, and in having centered it on the problem of freedom, revolt, and nonconformity.

This paper deals only with some of the aspects of modern art and literature. It goes without saying that a series of specific and rather precise sociological and aesthetic inquiries in depth must be developed. It might then be possible to establish a synthesis. And much more important, perhaps someday a society will arise where the problem of authentic art will no longer be merely the problem of refusal, but also that of acceptance: of men's entrance into a truly human society which can open the doors to hope.

4. INTERDEPENDENCIES BETWEEN INDUSTRIAL SOCIETY AND NEW FORMS OF LITERARY CREATION*

Recent works in the sociology of culture, especially those taking Georg Lukács' early studies as a starting point, have completely overturned the traditional conception of the relations between social life and artistic and literary creation. They have dealt with Western Europe since the 13th century and have shown, at least for that period, that artistic and literary creation was the imaginary transposition, at an extremely advanced level of coherence, of what I have called "world views": that is, ensembles of mental categories which tended towards coherent structures and which were proper to certain privileged social groups whose thought, feeling, and behavior were oriented toward an overall organization of interhuman relations and of relations between men and nature.

Traditional literary sociology and a great deal of contemporary academic sociology conceives the relations between social life and literary creation in the form of the *influence* of collective consciousness on a writer who reflects it in a more or less transposed manner. On the contrary, the research to which I am referring, including my own work, conceives social life as an ensemble of collective structuration processes oriented, as much on the psychic plane as on that of action, towards creating equilibria in the relations among men, and between men and nature. These structuration processes are expressed in the psyche of all the group's members; and within them cultural and especially literary creation have a privileged status

---

*This essay was written in 1965 and is published for the first time in this volume.

insofar as they elaborate universes which, while corresponding to the structuration tendencies of the group's mental categories (and thus to the consciousness of all its members),[1] nonetheless present an incomparably more advanced degree of coherence than the latter attain. Thus situated at a very advanced level of this internal unity toward which all members of the group more or less successfully tend, literary creation fulfills two essential functions in social life.

On the one hand, it must not reflect collective consciousness or merely record reality. Rather, creating on the imaginary plane a universe whose content may differ entirely from that of collective consciousness but whose structure is akin or even homologous to its structuration, it must help men gain awareness of themselves and of their own affective, intellectual, and practical aspirations. On the other hand, it simultaneously affords the group's members a satisfaction on the imaginary plane which must and can compensate for the multiple frustrations caused by the inevitable compromises and inconsistencies which reality imposes.

In this respect the creation of literature, art, philosophy, and so forth, fulfills a collective function which is at once analogous to and very unlike the individual function of the imaginary which Freud shed light on (slips, dreams, fantasies, etc.). The analogy holds insofar as in both cases it is a matter of compensations for the frustrations reality imposes, compensations which in the non-pathological case are destined to facilitate insertion into real life. But the individual frustrations Freud analyzed bear on the *content* of desire, on the objects which could satisfy it; whereas the collective frustrations for which cultural creation must compensate rarely and only subsidiarily bear on the content of collective desires, bearing more often and always essentially on the fundamental need for *coherence and totality* which characterizes all human, social life.

In this general framework, another important result of this recent sociological work is the establishment of a fundamental transformation in the relation between social life and literary creation beginning with the development of production for the market—which means, practically, beginning with capitalism.[2]

---

1. Because the group has no existence beyond the individuals composing it and the relations established between them and the surrounding world.

2. To simplify terminology in this study, the different historical stages of capitalist society are designated by four terms whose approximate value is acknowledged, but which can nonetheless be used heuristically without misunderstanding: rising capitalism (the 17th and 18th centuries, in France), liberal capitalism (19th century), monopoly and trust capitalism (first half of the 20th century), and organizational capitalism (the contemporary era, since WWII).

The relation between society and cultural creation continues to be of the type described for cultural creation in precapitalist societies, and also for valid works linked to capitalist societies' economic sector, which remains quantitatively predominant for a long time. It is a process of structuration of a collective consciousness: the categorial ensemble is being constituted. Whether elaborating a philosophical system or an imaginary universe of individual beings and particular situations, the creator transposes it onto the plane of conceptual thought or imaginary creation, pushing it to a very advanced degree of coherence. Thus the work preserves a character at once collective and individual. The group alone can elaborate a categorial ensemble oriented toward coherence, a world view; but it only very rarely—practically, almost never—brings it to the level of coherence attained in the *oeuvre*. The individual alone achieves that, and expresses it in a specific content.

In this perspective culture, and more precisely every important cultural work, appears as the highest-level meeting point of group and individual life. Its essence is to raise collective consciousness to a degree of unity toward which it was spontaneously oriented but might never have attained in empirical reality without the intervention of creative individuality. This situation is appreciably modified, however, by the appearance of production for the market and of what I will call the economic sector of social life.[3]

In relation to all the other forms of social life, this sector possesses a particular character fraught with consequences for creation. The thorough study of this problem would require more than a volume. I cannot dwell on it at length but will mention only the two most important traits characterizing the operation of the economic sector: a) Within the society as a whole, it tends to become an autonomous structure, submitting less and less to the influence of the other sectors of social life while exercising a growing influence upon them. That is, it tends to reduce the status of consciousness to that of a simple reflex (without entirely succeeding, of course). b) It eliminates all consciousness of transindividual (moral, religious, or historical) values from its domain and functioning, and allows only the universal value of the individual's autonomy to survive—and that only in the liberal period. Thus it transfers the functions which transindividual values had in all other forms of social life to a new

---

3. To avoid any misunderstanding it should be stressed that the economic is defined by the "existence of production for the market." Every other type of production, circulation, and distribution of goods depends on the sociological and the technological.

attribute (whose origin is purely social) of goods as commodities: to exchange value, price.

But beyond the suppression of any consciousness of supra-individual values *within economic life*, the economic sector's increasingly unilateral influence on the entire society of course tends to weaken the presence and operation of those values in the ensemble of social life. Above all, it tends to reduce their authenticity to the status of false consciousness, pure subjectivity, or even twaddle. Described in many well-known studies, this is the phenomenon of *reification*.

In recent years sociologists of literature have raised the importance of reification in understanding certain modern novels: from Kafka to Camus' *The Stranger*, Sartre' *Nausea*, Beckett's novels, and the contemporary New Novel. These efforts hold undeniable interest, but seem to me insufficient insofar as they do not address the problem of the stages of reification and of their differential influence on the process of literary creation. Chiefly, they do not see that, far from beginning only in the 20th century, reification has had repercussions on literary creation since the beginnings of commercial capitalism. Of course, these repercussions were initially localized and partial; and the most important seems to have been the appearance in literary life of a new genre destined for an illustrious future: the novel genre or, more precisely, the novel of the problematic hero.

Recently[4] I have tried to demonstrate a rigorous homology between the reified structure of the liberal market and this novel form, whose universe, like the market's, is characterized among other things by the absence of manifest transindividual values. Nonetheless, implicitly and through absence, these values structure a universe composed of two elements between which there is a dialectical relation of community and opposition: the degraded world ignorant of these values, and the hero who is himself degraded in a different way and pursues them in a problematic, mediated, non-conscious manner. Like the liberal economy, the universe of the classical novel recognizes only one explicit value: the individual and his development in a world at once familiar and strange to him. Thus the novel is *at once* a biography and a social chronicle.

Moreover, this homology is strengthened by a very extended analogy between the major turning points in the histories of the economy and of novel creation: a) Between the transition from the

---

4. *Pour une sociologie du roman* (Paris: Gallimard, Collection Idées, 1964).

liberal economy to that of cartels and monopolies, and the dissolution of the novel character; and b) Between the transition to organizational capitalism, and the appearance of the New Novel.

But these analogies between the structure and respective histories of exchange and the novel seem to correspond to a fundamental modification in the nature of the relation between the work and the society with which it is connected. The new characteristics of this relation can be schematically summarized in two points: a) The homology no longer operates through the collective consciousness of any group whatever, since it is impossible to find a third homologous or similar structure at the level of this consciousness. b) The work no longer represents the meeting point between individual and collective consciousness at the highest point attained by each, as it did earlier; but, on the contrary, represents a much more complex, more dialectical relation. The classical novel's universe has a structure relatively homologous to that governing the universe of men's everyday life in the economic sector, which is also thematically dominated by the only manifest, universal value of the liberal economy: the individual's autonomy and development. But from this common base the work of art and society evolve in different directions; and the work of art becomes the expression not of the social group but of a resistance to it, or at least of the non-acceptance of it.

These two complementary modifications in the relation between society and novelistic creation result, among other things, in the classical novel's inability to admit of a positive hero.[5] This inability is easy to explain insofar as such a hero would have to embody precisely the explicit values which govern the work's universe; whereas we have said that in the novel these values are entirely implicit, and never have a manifest character. In turn, this phenomenon is explained by the novel's linkage with the economy, which also renders all transindividual values implicit in its domain; and simultaneously by the absence of intermediary structures in collective consciousness which is merely its natural consequence. Tending to suppress all consciousness of supra-individual values, to render their operation implicit and to mediate it through exchange value, the economy can no longer act on literary creation through the intermediary of a collective consciousness which it tends precisely to

5. A positive hero is understood as a character who consciously embodies the values governing the work's universe in his thinking and his acts. Examples are Don Rodriguez, Horace, Andromaque, Junie, etc.

suppress. Thus we return to the starting point and can close the circle, recalling that the presence of a positive hero is excluded by the absence of a structure in collective consciousness homologous to the structure of exchange and by the absence of explicit, manifest supra-individual values in the novel's universe.[6]

Thus not merely in particular cases but as a literary genre, the classical novel most eloquently expressed its simultaneously realistic and critical character in the absence of the positive hero. This idea cannot be adequately developed in the framework of this study; I will restrict myself to stating that it allows us to understand why, although in precapitalist societies culture and especially literary works could be linked to an oppositional or even revolutionary group and could therefore take a negative attitude toward society (for example, 17th century French tragedy), they nonetheless never expressed an opposition between the individual and the social group to which they were connected. With the appearance and development of exchange and the literary genre connected with it,

---

6. For literary history as a whole the phenomenon is actually much more complex. There is also a novel genre which corresponds to the explicit values of bourgeois consciousness, but which on the whole remained at the stage of its sub-literature: the only important exceptions seem to be certain novels of the first half of the 19th century such as those of Eugène Sue, Victor Hugo, and especially Balzac. In this regard, in my last work I expressed the hypothesis that Balzac's work "may constitute the sole great literary expression of the universe structured by conscious bourgeois values: the individualism, thirst for power, money, and eroticism which overcame the old feudal values..." Cf. "Introduction to the Problems of a Sociology of the Novel," trans. Beth Blumenthal, in *Telos* 18, (Winter 1973-74), p. 133. In this perspective I observed that if this hypothesis proves to be accurate it could be linked with the fact that Balzac's work occurs precisely in the era when individualism—in itself ahistorical—structured the consciousness of the bourgeoisie which was constructing a new society.

I have formulated the hypothesis that four factors converge in the exchange structure's action on the novel's structure (this action does not pass through the link of collective consciousness): a) the category of mediation and the tendency to consider the approach to all values from the viewpoint of this category, which arises in the thought of members of bourgeois society from economic behavior and from the existence of exchange value; b) the subsistence of a certain number of problematic individuals in this society whose thought and behavior remain dominated by qualitative values, even though they cannot entirely shield these values from the general action of degrading mediation (in particular, this is the case for creators); c) the development of a non-conceptualized affective discontent and an affective aspiration aimed directly toward qualitative values, whether this occurs in the entire society or only among the middle strata from which most novelists are recruited; d) the existence in this society of liberal individualist values which, although not transindividual, nonetheless have a universal aim. These values engendered by bourgeois society contradict the important limitations that society brings to bear on possibilities for individual development.

For a more complete discussion see *Ibid.*, pp. 131-2.

the novel of the problematic hero, a great literary form appears which for the first time expresses by its very nature an opposition between the creative individual and the social group in which the categories structuring his work are elaborated.

In the classical novel, however, although this rupture was essential and profound it was not yet total. A fundamental value was still recognized and accepted as much in economic life as in the novel's universe: the value of the individual. The opposition lies in the novelist's realistic statement that this society, which preaches individual autonomy and development, nevertheless negates them in practice by the process of reification and by the conventional, deceptive, inhuman character of social structures. This new, antagonistic relation between the universe of the literary work and the social group will be accentuated in the history of Western literature. And corresponding to the very extent of that accentuation and of the economic sector's growing importance in the entire society, it will tend to transcend the framework of novelistic creation and to extend to other domains of cultural life, even to its entirety.

The first decisive turning point in the process occurs on the eve of WWI. On the economic plane, this is the era of qualitative transition in the process of concentration of capital from the liberal economy to the economy of cartels, monopolies, and trusts. Its corollary is the suppression of the liberal economy's only universal value: individual autonomy. In the history of the novel, it is the homologous turning point expressed in the dissolution of the character and the tendency toward the disappearance of the hero. But this conjoint suppression of the individual's structural importance in the economy and in the novel *eliminates precisely the only explicit common value* and breaks the last conscious, manifest bond between the novel and society.

As I have shown elsewhere, this transition occurs through many forms of novelistic creation, whether they correspond to the dissolution of the character or to the attempt to replace it with collective subjects (families, institutions, revolutionary groups, etc.). These attempts have undoubtedly created important works, but they did not issue in any lasting continuations. The major line of evolution proceeds essentially from Joyce through Kafka, Camus' *The Strnager* and Jean-Paul Sartre's *Nausea*, to the recent novels of Beckett, Nathalie Sarraute, and Alain Robbe-Grillet. Moreover, this time the critical attitude toward society and toward the ensemble of groups constituting it is no longer specific to the novel.

During the first period of commercial capitalism, in the 17th century, and during the 19th century period of liberal capitalism, the development of production for the market eliminated supra-individual (transcendent or historical) values from the consciousness of individuals in the economic sector, and considerably weakened them in all other sectors. It replaced these values, which had founded all earlier Western cultural creation, with the universal value of the individual, which permitted the development of great classical philosophy in its two major currents: rationalism and empiricism, and, in 18th century France, their temporary synthesis in Enlightenment philosophy. But whereas philosophical thought resolutely accepted individual consciousness and its autonomy as a starting point, literary creation continued the old cultural tradition which seeks the person's ultimate basis in the supra-individual. Thus, the latter being reduced to implicitness, it gave rise to the creation of the novel of the problematic hero, which expressed the contradiction between the creative personality—or even mere personality—and the conventional, reified character of individualist society.

The transition from the liberal economy to the economy of trusts and monopolies entailed the suppression of the foundations of individualism, and created a situation where philosophy and literature could no longer be founded either on transindividual values long since reduced to implicitness or on the individual's autonomy and development. The only remaining foundation for philosophy and literature was the dissolution of individual and global structures and its concomitant, the limit—and especially the limit *par excellence*, death. On this basis, the temporarily different orientations of individualist philosophy and literature in the classical period yielded to a conjoint evolution in which the novels of Kafka, Sartre, and Camus correspond to an important philosophical current, existentialism, itself centered on absence, the absurd, anguish, and death. From the outset, the novel of the problematic hero was the literary form of the *absence* of supra-individual values, and of the insufficiency of the individualist universe where the self could not be founded on conscious acceptance of such values. It now continues in the much more radical form of total absence and dissolution, and of the sensibility of anguish which allies it with existentialist philosophy. (Sartre, in this era the philosopher as well as the writer of this perspective, is highly characteristic.)

The end of the war of 1939-1945 marks a new turning point in the history of Western capitalism. Whatever their orientation, sociologists have established it in designating contemporary society by a whole series of specific terms intended to indicate this transformation: mass society, consumer society, or organizational capitalism. The changes in relation to the period of trust and monopoly capitalism are remarkable and, of course, have important cultural repercussions.

First, the period between 1910 and 1947-1948 was marked by extremely unstable, continually threatened economic equilibria. Capitalist society could be maintained only through considerable national and international shocks (two world wars, the Russian revolution, the defeat of several European revolutions, fascism, Nazism, the 1929-1933 crisis, the Spanish Civil War). The instability of an equilibrium which was destroyed and provisionally re-established each time (Marxists called it the crisis of capitalism) lay at the base of the *malaise* and the sensibility of anguish which characterized the era's two great cultural creations, existentialist philosophy and the novel of the dissolution of the character (but which can, of course, be recognized in many other domains).

Today this period is definitively over, and has given way to a dynamic and relatively stable equilibrium. The cultural super-structures corresponding to the earlier period are also being surpassed, even though some great literary manifestations are still connected with it. (It suffices to mention the writings of Bechett and Nathalie Sarraute; moreover, sociologists know that to a greater or lesser extent cultural creations outlive the socioeconomic realities in which they develop.) On the philosophical plane, existentialism has also become part of history. Anguish disappeared even in Heidegger's last works; and the contemporary era's dominant philosophy seems to be bound up with a rationalism which insists much less on the individual's autonomy than on the permanence of structures. The success of structuralist linguistics is highly symptomatic: there a cultural and ideological phenomenon far surpasses the undeniable scientific and methodological interest which the development of this science holds. Similarly, on the literary plane the New Novel, at least in the first period, began by presenting a universe where man is entirely subordinate to things and whose structure and mechanisms it analyzed realistically and pitilessly, but almost entirely without anguish.

Besides this disappearance of anguish, the behavior and psychic structure of men in Western industrial societies underwent another great change (established and studied in some remarkable sociological analyses, especially by David Riesman and Juergen Habermas). In this society, where the individual's importance and autonomy has entirely disappeared in economic life but economic and social equilibrium is reconstituted in a relatively solid way, the great majority of men become essentially consumers, especially on the psychic plane.

An entire sector of their intellectual and affective life is progressively reduced and severely diminished. This sector still played a major role during the liberal and imperialist periods, and was constituted by concerns linked to productive activities, to the social and political organization of the entire society, to problems of general interest, and hence to comprehension of and participation in cultural life. A type of man arises whose psychic structure is essentially passive, who is estranged from all responsible decisions, and who is oriented essentially toward consumption (which, of course, also includes the ensemble of leisure and cultural consumption).

However, reading a book or seeing a play in order to find a problematic in it—a stance which is accepted or refused in a relation of intellectual exchange—is essentially different from reading the same book or watching the same spectacle from the purely consumer perspective of leisure and distraction.

What is disappearing is the public opinion which in the two preceding periods was constituted in law by all the citizens, but was constituted in fact by a relatively thin stratum of more or less cultivated people, bourgeois, and members of the middle classes—especially of the liberal and intellectual professions. For the writer, this stratum—or, if you will, this relatively large elite—as a whole constituted a sort of intermediate nourishing soil between the entire society and cultural creation.

Today the writer confronts a society which massively consumes all sorts of goods, including, eventually, his own books. But at best, this consumption can assure him a relatively high income and, in a rather small number of privileged cases, can allow him to lead a certain way of life. Insofar as it no longer constitutes an active participation in economic, social, and political life, and implicitly in cultural creation, however, this consumption can only provide the writer increasingly less help in forming his consciousness and developing his personal character and work.

In these conditions the rupture between creator and society overstepped the novel's limits, initially giving rise to an avant-garde theater whose essential content was above all the declaration of the disappearance of all community among men, even on the immediate level of communication. Such is Ionesco's early theater up to *Rhinoceros*, Adamov's early theater, Beckett's, and also two of the most remarkable plays in modern drama, Genet's *The Balcony* and Gombrowicz's *The Marriage*: in the imaginary, these plays transpose all the historical experience of the last forty years and terminate in a closed universe of nightmare and absence of communication.

At the same time, what is currently called the New Novel appeared on the plane of novelistic creation. It describes a perfectly structured, equilibrated, autonomous universe where, however, the deformed, flattened human is entirely dominated and is obliterated to the limit by inert objects, which now take the primary role and become the true active elements of this universe. Successively analyzing Robbe-Grillet's novels and films, I have been able to show the extent to which the theme of almost every one of these works is a fundamental structural law or trait of contemporary Western industrial societies and its contribution to the destruction of man.[7]

Finally, the New Novel's problematic has recently penetrated the cinema; several films reveal the same character: especially Godard's *Contempt*, Resnais' *Muriel*, Resnais and Robbe-Grillet's *Last Year at Marienbad*, and Robbe-Grillet's *L'Immortelle*.[8] And in painting, the development of non-figurative painting since the beginning of the century, and the disappearance of man and his familiar universe, are certainly phenomena connected with those already described; a more thorough study could probably distinguish analogous stages.

This whole ensemble of creations seems to occur within a process of radicalization which began with the novel of the problematic hero, continued in existentialist philosophy and the novel of the dissolution of character in a decomposed, anguished world, and issued in the reappearance of a stable, balanced, but rigorously ahuman universe. This time, on the structural plane, the rupture becomes radical. It is located no longer only on the plane of values, but on that of language.

I do not believe this is a matter of a current phenomenon, a new style which is hard to understand in its initial appearance and requires some time to become accessible to the reader. The difficulty of comprehending abstract painting, the books of Beckett, Genet, or Gombrowicz, and the novels of Robbe-Grillet or Claude Ollier,

---

7. *The Erasers* describes a process of internal self-regulation which ends in the daily murder of a citizen; *The Voyeur*, men's general passivity, which allows murder to be integrated naturally into the novel's universe; *Jealousy*, the total reification of human realities and the assimilation of the human to objects; *Last Year at Marienbad*, the reversal of the structure of time—the fact that the future determines the past—which corresponds to an economic transformation in a society of planning and the total absence of hope; *L'Immortelle*, the conflict between the world and the imaginary, and the impossibility of reconciling them. See the more detailed analyses in *Ibid.*, and in Anne Olivier and Lucien ̣dmann, "*L'Immortelle* est de retour" in *France-Observateur*, no. 751, 24 September 1964, pp. 15-16.

8. See Annie Goldmann, *Cinéma et société moderne* (Paris: Editions Anthropos, 1971).

could be compared instead to that which men accustomed to seeing the sun revolve around the Earth experienced when they abruptly had to learn that the reverse was true. That message has finally been assimilated, and today men admit the scientific truth; but on this point their consciousness nonetheless remains split into two different sectors: that of everyday life, where Earth is immobile and the sun revolves through the sky, and that of known truth. In literature, this is somewhat like the situation of Ionesco's plays: the spectators have already more or less assimilated them and understand them when they see them on stage; but they usually do not seriously imagine that the spectacle might have any relation to their everyday life. For lack of a code which would allow the reader or spectator to recognize their intellectual content, however, the other works I have mentioned are not yet assimilable. Although plays like *The Balcony* and films like *Muriel* have a certain success, it is primarily for purely affective reasons, without any intellectual comprehension of their content having intervened. In fact, the total absence of man's responsibility in modern technocratic society still creates an affective *malaise* in many individuals which constitutes a sort of background of their existence and is a definitive form of integration into that society. This non-conceptualized *malaise* is what spectators and readers believe they recognize in Resnais' films and in certain writings whose content they assimilate poorly.

The problem of future perspectives arises here. It seems certain that by dissolving the intermediate, active groups which were the constitutive elements of a collective creative consciousness during earlier periods of Western capitalist society, modern Western society—whatever we call it—is creating a social structure capable of integrating most of its members. Increasingly, a void is created between, on the one hand, families composed of individuals whose decision-making functions tend to disappear, who more and more become mere functionaries, and whose psychic activity is thus entirely structured by consumption, and, on the other hand, the overall society—especially the State. This void permits the existence only of pressure groups aiming to influence the State so as to procure a rising standard of living for their members. This evolution presents a clear danger for cultural creation. On one side, there is doubtless a rise in the level of knowledge, a massive consumption of information and imaginative works (paperback books tend to assimilate even literature to the mass media). On the other side, there is a literary creation which is the act of individuals who are undeniably integrated into practical life, and often lead an easy but increasingly marginal, isolated existence as creators in the midst of a society which affords them an increasingly less nourishing soil to fertilize and promote their creation. Of course I am not about to make prognoses, especially since the future of cultural creation depends primarily on these societies' social and economic evolution, which has not been entirely completed. In conclusion, however, it can be said that the crisis in contemporary avant-garde Western literature is grave; writers have a difficult time staying on the increasingly narrow path which contemporary society still allows them, and they have already begun turning toward romanticism and the literature of evasion.

The novel was a classical genre. Today in France we have not only a hallowed, right-thinking romantic novelist like Montherlant but also an important avant-garde novelist, Marguerite Duras, whose work has an entirely romantic character. Since *Rhinoceros*, Ionesco has replaced radical criticism with an almost didactic moralism; Sartre and Robbe-Grillet each end their last work of fiction with a suicide. In *L'Immortelle*, Robbe-Grillet poses the problem of choice between the world and the imaginary, between evasion and romanticism: this choice reveals the extent to which the great tradition of realist and classical literature, which developed on the basis first of ancient, then Christian, and finally bourgeois and secular humanism, is in a decisive crisis today.

The great socialist thinkers foresaw this crisis and hoped to oppose it with a humanist culture linked to the development of the revolutionary proletariat. In this respect the evolution of Western industrial societies has dealt them a cruel disappointment. The proletariat has ended up more or less integrated into capitalist societies which, after a long period of crisis, have found a relatively stable equilibrium and today have reached an exceptional pace and level of economic vigor. On the social plane, however, the technocratic societies being constituted as corollaries of this evolution are composed of a thin stratum of directors who make almost all the important decisions, and a mass of administered functionaries who come to be assured a continual rise in their standard of living and an increasing consumption, but who participate less and less actively in social, political, and cultural life. As Marx and later Marxist theoreticians foresaw, these societies are proving to be a considerable, perhaps mortal threat to humanism and to creation.

5. DIALECTICAL THOUGHT
AND TRANSINDIVIDUAL SUBJECT*

Ten years ago I probably would have apologized for having to employ such apparently forbidding terms as transindividual subject, structure, or function. Today, on the contrary, I should apologize for being pedestrian, for only using some words which have become common and for avoiding an entire terminology which, finally—although I have nothing against neologisms required to clarify thought—seems to me too often superfluous.

Every philosophical exposition begins, of course, with a starting point which cannot be proved: if it were proved it would not be a starting point. All the same, it has to be justified; but it can be justified only at the end. One can begin with the *cogito* or with sensation. Attempting to think in a perspective of dialectic and of positive research as well, I begin from a different starting point, which I hope will be justified in the course of the exposition: the claim that if we want to do positive research, all radical duality must be categorically rejected as contrary to positive reality, to the empirical givens, and to the positive explanation of facts. As I will try to show with some quotations, this radical duality characterizes a great deal of contemporary thought. In opposition to that attitude, I think that any radical duality is ideological and that the only way to grasp the facts, to comprehend social reality, consists

*Originally published in *Bulletin de la Société française de Philosophie*, vol. 64, no. 3, July-September 1970.

precisely of seeing the partial, relative, operative justification of this duality and the danger represented by the idea of making it total, radical, and absolute.

The first dualities I want to question are that of philosophy and science, and that of theory and *praxis*. For an entire long-standing philosophical position, philosophy is only the attempt to think the ensemble of the universe in a rational, closed fashion, or at least to begin from the subject in speculatively creating a global, closed, coherent vision. Opposing this view is a positivist conception of science according to which a science becomes positive precisely when it frees itself from philosophy, when it consists only of the most precise empirical recording of facts and correlations possible. From this conception an entire position develops, which pretends it is science and can completely free itself from philosophical reflection.

I do not believe this duality is acceptable: first of all in the perspective of science and its requirements, very simply because this conception of science wants to record facts in the indicative, to reproduce an objective reality, but thus implicitly comes to forget who is recording. Clearly, however, we record facts with a conceptual apparatus which is not abstract and which we ourselves have not created. Although subjectively and logically one can proceed by recurrence back to the *cogito*, that very position—like every other one—is given within a civilization and is accepted by a man who finds himself in the world and deals with an ensemble of mental structures, categories, values, judgments, and criteria which he himself has not created but which are given him in the world he wants to comprehend. At the limit, this statement would be valid even for the natural sciences; but the status they have gained today is such that the perspective they work in can be said to be valid for *all* men in advanced industrial civilizations, and potentially for all who could or might want to attain that level. With the human sciences the situation changes because particular perspectives (I hope to offer some examples), valorizations, and specific structurations are entirely predominant.

I do not in the least want to end up in a relativism, because I think there are precise criteria which can allow us to be as scientific as possible provided we recognize the difficulties and see precisely where we are situated. In any case, the subject's structuration, the specific structuration of the subject's mental categories with which he perceives and organizes reality in his research, is of course one of the most important elements of his work's validity. Working in the human sciences without reflecting on the researcher's condition, on the perspectives in which he works, and on the very problematic of those sciences, is to risk falling into positivism and taking for *the* truth what is only a partial aspect of *a* truth. It is to do work which can have scientific value only insofar as one is aware of this situation and can address the problem of its limitation and its overcoming. The object of study—society, for the human sciences—is found within the subject, whatever it be, even if here we hold provisionally to the idea of the particular, individual subject. Clearly, when a writer writes a history of the French Revolution today he does so with values partially created by the French Revolution; it could not be imagined that he simply does objective science without taking account of his position relative to that Revolution—of the fact that the object of his study is within himself. If on the other hand the subject is an important thinker (it will soon be seen whether, as I think, it is a social group), then insofar as he forms part of the object of study he is not situated outside it. He and all who read him transform and consciously grasp a certain attitude, a certain ensemble of statements which, to the extent certain men or human groups are convinced of their truth, appear to be truths; and this implies a change of the object: subject and object are not radically separable. One can and must try to introduce a maximum of critical spirit, which means, however, that the human sciences cannot be done as though from the viewpoint of divinity or the absolute. All discourse on the absolute is conducted from a position within the world, a relative position; and it can have no more pretension of presenting itself as the truth than any other claim about social, empirical reality. To do positive science in the human sciences we are obliged to be philosophical: to reflect on the status of knowledge, on the status of the knowing subject, and on its place in the elaboration of truths.

The same situation appears where the relation between theory and practice is concerned. Insofar as science is a knowledge of the world which not only permits its transformation but also, in the domain of the human sciences, transforms society by its mere development (society is no longer the same if collective thought changes), it is not a matter of affirming a radical separation of theory and *praxis*. In the moment when we think, with all our aspirations, and with our entire problematic, we form part of society; clearly every development of a theoretical claim has a practical character and transforms social reality in one direction or another, to a more or less developed degree. It seems questionable to affirm the break between theory and praxis, or even to claim that theory is objective and *praxis* is only its application.

I will try to address the problem of the subject in this perspective. In the contemporary human sciences, the great fashion, asserted by an entire important school, is to proclaim that the subject is a prejudice of the last century or of earlier schools, and that present science must dispense with it. As well, it is claimed that from Descartes to Sartre by way of Husserl, the subject has always been conceived as an individual subject. Therefore, before addressing the problem of the concept of the subject in scientific research and the conditions making this concept indispensable to comprehension, I want to establish its status insofar as possible in a few words.

Of course, the subject is no more an objective given than the facts. Facts are *constructed*, first within the thought process and already in perception (everyone knows the psychologists' work, especially Piaget's). But even outside immediate perception, up to the most elaborate theories, the facts are constructions. These constructions, however, are not arbitrary: they have a reason for existing and are founded on the possibility of orientation, of helping to comprehend and transform the world; they are not mere givens external to the thinker. The concept of the subject, of course, has the same status as all other scientific concepts: it is a construction, but a grounded one. Insofar as this concept is a construction we must ask what it consists of and what its function is: what is its necessity, utility, and role in factual research, in the study of empirical facts?

I would like to propose the initial thesis that the subject has the function of rendering the facts we propose to study intelligible and comprehensible. It is a question of knowing their nature and knowing how they can be comprehended in their reciprocal relations, in the empirical characters they present to observation, and in their genesis and becoming: how these facts which did not always exist appeared one day, were transformed, and subsequently disappeared or—if the present society is in question—are still being transformed.

But what characterizes the two positions on the subject—the subject conceived as individual, conscious, and privileged (at least in consciousness, if it is not reducible to consciousness), and contemporary structuralism's negation of the subject—is that they are two corresponding and complementary limitations. The position which begins with the individual subject will not be able to account for the relationship among phenomena, for their character of being structured, being an ensemble. Inversely, the negation of the subject does not successfully account for the becoming or genesis of structure. In the perspective of these two limitations, I would like to say a few words about the structuralist school, which is now developing and is assuming an extremely important position in research in the contemporary human sciences.

For a very long time the sciences and philosophy were dominated by the idea of the individual subject: for example, by the existentialist thought of Sartre, who, even in the texts he thinks most reconciled with Marxism, retains as his fundamental starting point the organic subject, the perceiving individual. During this long period, the dialectical perspective constantly had to maintain the existence not only of structures external to the subject which constituted limitations of possible choice, but also of structures internal to the subject which made him able to think only in a certain way, made certain forms of thought inaccessible to him and incapable of being developed. Inversely, after the development of the linguistic type of structuralism, for us it is precisely a matter of showing the extent to which facts are incomprehensible without the concept of the subject, which this school tries to eliminate at any cost.

Most contemporary structuralist systems are immediately characterized by the elimination of that concept to which the idea of the subject is essentially linked: functionality. I will take a single example. Lévi-Strauss' passage on Marx is a radical misunderstanding (Althusser's texts contain exactly the same idea). Lévi-Strauss refers to a famous text of Marx in the preface to the *Contribution to the Critique of Political Economy*, and thinks his own position is close to Marxism: "I do not postulate a kind of pre-existent harmony between the different levels of structure. They may be—and often are—in mutual contradiction, but the modes of contradiction all belong to the same type. And indeed, this is what historical materialism teaches, asserting that it is always possible to proceed, by transformation, from the economic structure or that of social relations to the structure of law, art, or religion. But Marx never claimed that these transformations were all of a single type—for example, that ideology could only reflect social relations like a mirror. In his view, these transformations are dialectical, and in some cases he went to great lengths to discover the crucial transformation... If we grant, following Marx's thought, that infrastructures and superstructures are made up of multiple levels and that there are various types of transformations..."[1]

But Marx's corresponding text is very precise: he speaks not, as Lévi-Strauss' interpretation would have it, of transformation or inversion between infrastructure and superstructure, but instead of *functionality*: "At a certain stage of development, the material productive forces of society come into conflict with the existing relations of production or—this merely expresses the same thing in legal terms—with the property relations within the framework of which they have operated hitherto. From forms of development of the productive forces these relations turn into their fetters."[2]

Essential to the relationship between relations of production and means of production is not that they are homologous or inverse, or that by certain transformation rules one can obtain the transition from one to the other. The relation is of a very precise type: that of favoring or being an element in the development of men's behavior or, inversely, of being a fetter. The great difference between contemporary structuralism and the dialectical positions is precisely that structuralism rejects any concept of functionality.

Some reservations must be made about the following image since it comes, for the moment, from an individual example; but what Marx says is fairly close to this. If, for example, for reasons of productivity or demeanor I had to hit this table with a hammer, and if I found myself lying on the ground, then I would tend to get up since my upright posture is more functional than the lying position and better facilitates the act of hitting the table. If men must produce with the windmill or with modern industry, certain relations of production are more functional than others and better permit fulfilling the task. Of course, there are homologies between the relations and functionalities within superstructures—we constantly work with these relations of homology and there is no question of eliminating them. But modern structuralism's so-called Marxist interpretation is characterized by the replacement of functionality (Althusser even says *combinatoire* when he translates this text) with relations of homology, inversion, or transformation. That is, it eliminates the subject and its specific function, which is to account for functionality and intelligibility. Basically, in the human sciences today, I believe the concept of functionality is the most exact, precise form corresponding to what was formerly and

---

1. *Structural Anthropology*, trans. Claire Jacobson and Brooks Grundfest Schoepf, (New York: Basic Books, Inc., 1963), p. 333, translation modified.
2. *A Contribution to the Critique of Political Economy*, trans. S.W. Ryazanskaya (New York: International Publishers, 1970), p. 21.

much more approximately called meaning . An entire philosophy of consciousness saw meaning only in the end, in comprehension, in intelligibility. To take a banal example, when a cat catches a mouse its behavior is *functional*; it can be translated in terms of problem and solution; there is a disequilibrium which must be resolved: that does not presuppose consciousness.

When men act, consciousness is always present; but there is no reason to concede—it is not even probable—that this consciousness is always perfectly adequate: it is one element of behavior. Very often it may be adequate, just as it may be inadequate or more or less adequate. What matters is that men's behavior is functional and as such meaningful,[3] exactly like the behavior of the cat catching a mouse.

Lévi-Strauss calls it a truism to say that a society functions, and an absurdity to say that everything functions (or something similar). The problem, though, is not to say that every society functions, which would in fact be a truism, but instead to know *how* it functions: this is extremely important, and it is precisely what the human sciences study. But there is more. The idea that everything is functional is at the basis of all dialectical thought—and in the specific case this means Marx's thought as much as Freud's (I will shortly try to establish the differences between them). A sociological school rather imprecisely calling itself structural functionalism does exist (Parsons and that whole group), and it works with the concept of the dysfunctional. There are dysfunctional realities as well, but they are dysfunctional only in relation to an existing society: everything is not functional for the existing society. If we ask why dysfunctional elements appear in this society or, on the psychoanalytic plane, in a biography, the only answer is precisely the one Marx gave in his preface to the *Contribution to the Critique of Political Economy*, and I see no other scientific answer: because men have meaningful reasons (which does not denote conscious elements) for behaving dysfunctionally in relation to that society. But this means that a new functionality is arising. Every phenomenon is dysfunctional or functional in relation to what exists; but when dysfunctional in relation to what exists, it becomes functional in relation to a society in becoming, to something in the process of transformation which because of opposition may never come into being, but which has a

---

3. Goldmann uses *sens* and *signification* interchangeably; both are translated as "meaning" [*Trans.*].

meaning for men's behavior. This meaning must be found: the duality between functionality and dysfunctionality is still one of the most problematic in scientific research. We must work in relation to a certain society but must know exactly what is dysfunctional in relation to the present: for example, what was dysfunctional in relation to feudal society—the development of the third estate and the bourgeoisie—was at the birth of a new functionality for an emerging society.

The attempt to create a positive human science is not the general, speculative statement that everything is functional, which is a truism, but instead the formulation of the problem in each confrontation with a concrete phenomenon: what is its structure, and what is that structure's functionality? If, as a whole, contemporary structuralism recognizes only partial structures, and eventually the order of orders and structure of structures which govern the remotest events and allow classifications, it is because structuralism eliminates the concepts of functionality, the subject, and transformation: the idea of history. Here I do not want to analyze the ideological motives at the basis of this elimination. What is important is simply to establish and demonstrate that structuralism has an implicitly nonscientific character, because its division of reality requires structuralism to leave aside a large part of it—a part which, moreover, is in evidence. When structuralists criticize Marxism or dialectical thought they say that for the "Hegelian, Lukácsian, or Kantian" Marxists, as they call them, everything is rigorously coherent; and that there is a single, entirely functional totality in which they, the structuralists, are constantly isolating and revealing partial structures, different domains, languages, kinships, and so forth. But this duality is as false as all the others I have mentioned. What is important is that each of these structures is bound to a subject, and that the subjects are not always essentially different. There is neither a single totality nor a single meaning of the entire society, nor inversely are there separate structural domains which allow many elements of reality to be left aside. Rather, there are men's behaviors, behaviors of subjects who create these structures out of functional, human needs. Thus we can see what could be linked together, what stands in the way, and what are the cooperations, oppositions, and laws of development.

In this perspective I now want to address the problem of the collective subject. I will address it anew at an extremely simple, banal level. I have said that the subject is what enables us to comprehend behaviors and thus realities and events. Take a very simple example. Pierre and I are lifting a particularly heavy chair and reflect a bit on who lifted it. Any system which begins with the *cogito* and the individual subject—which means a very large part of Western philosophy—cannot positively answer this question because it is Pierre and I who have lifted the chair. If we admit for an instant the relation between *praxis* and consciousness, the idea that I have lifted the chair, and that Pierre and the chair are the objects of my consciousness, rests on an illusion. It is a matter not of hypostatizing the collective subject, situating it somewhere outside individual consciousnesses, but instead of knowing that my consciousness of the world can be meaningful only if I take account of the fact that, beside me, Pierre's consciousness along with mine forms an ensemble which allows a behavior issuing in the act of lifting the chair. The complete subject of the action and, implicitly, the structure of consciousness, can be comprehended only by starting with the fact that men act together—that there is a division of labor.

This brings us to the problematic of the individual and collective subjects and their function in events. Clearly there are phenomena of the individual subject which modern psychology has shed light on; they are everything Freud designated as being of the order of the *libido*. In passing, I point out that Lévi-Strauss' terminology risks a confusion: because he has mentioned Freud, he uses "unconscious" to refer not only to the Freudian phenomena, but also to mental structures, permanent structures of mind, and the temporary structures which exist for a longer or shorter time. I prefer the term "non-conscious" because there is a radical difference between a repressed complex, which requires a whole psycho-analytic treatment or has to surmount an entire censorship to be restored to consciousness, and, for example, the laws of logic, which one is not conscious of if one has not learned logic. There are non-conscious phenomena which govern a part of behavior but which are other than the Freudian unconscious—they will be discussed. But finally, that said, there are phenomena of the individual subject, as Freud has shown, which account for a whole ensemble of behaviors: they have precisely the character of being comprehensible in their functionality and meaning in relation to an individual (consider the explications of dreams, slips, fantasy, and so forth). What I want to specify, however—and I will try to give a concrete example—is that all these phenomena which exist in each behavior and account for its individual and libidinal sector, to use Freud's term, cannot account for the sector linked to the social division of labor and hence to history. Leaving aside the modern psychoanalysis which tries to eliminate Freud's central idea that every phenomenon is meaningful in relation to a subject, the Freudian system's fundamental weakness is its attempt to account for historical phenomena on the basis of the individual subject. I do not want to discuss such attempts at social analysis in aesthetics; but I would like to give an example from aesthetic creation, a domain which even today, for most critical people, can seem to be linked with libidinal aspects.

During recent years we have worked on Genet's theater and writings, among other things. Everyone knows that homosexuality is involved in Genet's novels, in his first play, *Deathwatch*, and also in the army of *The Screens*. Here as in many other cases, this fact, which seems linked to the *libido*, has been facilely related to certain possible tendencies of the writer. But that permits absolutely no comprehension of Genet's works, as I will now try to show. From *The Maids* to *The Screens* we find heterosexual loves at the center of the plays: the Maids and the milkman, Monsieur and Madame, Vertu and Village, Chantal and Roger, · Said and his wife, are exquisite portrayals of heterosexual love; here homosexuality plays almost no role. Then how can this be related to the writer's unconscious, his *libido*, his deep tendencies? If we abandon any such attempt and analyze the work's structure and function in relation to the social group and the collective subject, we will have an answer which seems to me much closer to an empirical comprehension of the facts. Actually, we find that Genet's first writings, the novels and *Deathwatch*, are written in the perspective of a very precise collective subject: outsiders, petty thieves, prostitutes, and the whole world which is marginal in relation to society. The writings express this social group's perspective or vision. But nonconformism is the primary criterion of that perspective. Nonconformism is, in fact, being outside what society accepts. But this group does not elaborate its own values; and analyzing these writings reveals values accepted in society: friendship, love, courage, risk. A nonconformist novel could not be created with these elements; and everything which forms the aesthetic value of Genet's writings would no longer be found in these texts. For this reason all the values constituting Genet's novels have a double character, an oblique dimension which renders them nonconformist: love, but homosexual love; courage, but courage in crime. But when, after events familiar to all of us, Genet subsequently draws closer to the French left, to Sartre and

Les Temps Modernes, he begins to write plays with collective characters. With the conflict between oppressors and oppressed, between dominated and dominators, between the Maids and Monsieur and Madame, between the Blacks and the Whites, between the populace and the powerful, his texts are critical even in the very assertion of that conflict. He no longer needs the oblique dimension; and structuration, the aesthetic requirement of meaning and of rigorous functionality, leads to the disappearance of that dimension. Why does it reappear in the army of *The Screens?* Here again, the reason is an aesthetic one, concerning collective subjects rather than problems of individual biography. Genet's universe expresses the French left's perspective much better and more coherently than many of its representatives at the conceptual level. One of the essential ideas in this universe is that the populace represents human values in relation to the dominators, who appear as caricatures and mere puppets, but that this populace is weak and succeeds in expressing its value only on the spiritual plane, in the ritual celebrated by the Maids, the populace, or the Blacks. But when he writes the play of the victory of the dominated, *The Screens,* the vanquished army itself plays the ritual of combat: by the very fact that it has already lost the battle it threatens to be valorized. Since it is important for Genet that his play be nonconformist and not accomodate any external institution, all the oblique dimensions (and not just homosexuality) reappear in this part of the work.

The problem is thus to create a functional structure within the historical dimension; and to do so the writer of course makes use of what he knows, whether it be personal experience, books, or what he has learned. But the immediately established link with the individual subject is valid only apart from the facts. In reality, like the act of lifting the chair, every literary work is written in the historical perspective where men collaborate in the division of labor to create the external world and everything having a historical dimension—that is, implicitly, all of culture. For this reason a great work, which can be comprehended only in relation to a given collective subject (which is the method of explication), can be presented at the conclusion of research as having its own meaning. *Phèdre, Hamlet,* or a Genet play have a meaning of their own which I can isolate only by studying them within the social structures in which they arose and which explain how they were understood. Like the meaning of every cultural phenomenon, a play's own meaning is situated at two levels. In relation to the individual subject there is a libidinal meaning, but it is neither aesthetic nor historical: from the viewpoint of the individual subject, the writings of Racine or of whatever individual have the same meaning, explain certain problems, and are coherent in relation to the individual. The distinction between what corresponds to this subject and is functional for it, and what is not, can be made only through relation to the collective subject, the group, the transindividual subject. But what is important is that for the first time, in cultural questions this perspective can account for a complex of facts or empirical givens large enough that two explications with the same operative scientific value are impossible.

Again, I will take two series of examples at the sociological and literary levels, about which I will say at the outset that all attempts to study literary, cultural, or social facts with structuralist methods which eliminate functionality are susceptible to the same parallel, complementary criticisms I have mentioned. In this, moreover, I believe I am much more faithful to Saussure than is any linguistic structuralist. Saussure knew and said that the laws of language cannot be applied to speech: linguistic structuralism is valid for language but not for speech. Why? Because the functionality of language—communication—is universally human; whereas the functionality of speech always refers to a particular subject—it has a meaning. The French language is neither optimistic nor pessimistic because it must permit communication of optimism or pessimism, it must communicate enthusiasm or any other concrete communication; whereas speech always has a particular meaning. Literary, cultural, or social phenomena, the Club des jacobins, the student movement of May-June 1968, or any other historical fact; the behavior of the Bolsheviks during the Russian Revolution or of a certain group during a war: are these facts of language or facts of speech, in the sense in which speech is very specifically meaning or functionality in relation to the particular subject? In the very name of linguistics as Saussure formulated it, which seems valid to me, it is necessary to say that this structuralism, which can study only means, cannot study speech. Of course, speech utilizes means—language, in this particular case—but utilizes only a sector of it, an ensemble of elements, in order to realize a functionality or meaning. And if this functionality or meaning is eliminated, there is no possibility of explaining why these specific means have been utilized rather than others. By simply inventorying them, how can it be known whether these means are relevant or superfluous? Instead, if we work from the collective subject and take not merely consciousness but behavior into consideration, we can easily succeed in accounting entirely or almost completely for the facts when a text is in question, and in accounting for an incomparably larger portion of the facts when social reality is in question.

Here, first, is the example on the sociological level. It goes without saying that it cannot be situated on the single level of speech and of people's intention. Comprehending phenomena requires comprehending behavior and speeches, and simultaneously their functioning within a structure in relation to the collective subject. Take a rather important example, the attitude of the French capitalist, from one of our most famous sociologists. We learn that the capitalist has no very precise attitude: "[I]n the last ten years...I have met some representatives of capitalism, the 'cursed race,' and I have never known them to hold firm and unanimous opinions about the policy to be followed in Indochina, in Morocco, or in Algeria. I am ready to admit that a man with interests in a particular part of the world was open to argument. Even that banality is not entirely true. In matters concerning Morocco the 'big French capitalists' divided into two groups, one of which thought...and the other feared..."[4]

Judging a social group's behavior merely by asking individuals "What do you think?" forgetting that what people say does not simply correspond to what they do, confusing consciousness with overall functionality: this is an empiricist method which never allows comprehension of the reality of phenomena. Surely if one asks people what they think of an opposing group, one will get the most diverse opinions. It is necessary to integrate consciousness in behavior, to seek its meaning and its functionality, and the functionality of the two. Another of the same sociologist's theses concerns Trotsky's elimination by Stalin. We learn that the latter was general secretary of the Party, that he had a tactical superiority, etc.: "Perhaps it is not necessary to invoke the law of history to explain that in the end the party chose Stalin rather than Trotsky."[5]

Pardon me for believing that the problem occurs not on this level, but on the level of knowing why Stalin had become general secretary and why he had made the secretariat a decisive position. In the same way, historical factors such as the German defeat in

---

4. Raymond Aron, *Democracy and Totalitarianism*, trans. Valence Ionescu (London: Weidenfeld and Nicolson, 1968), p. 91, translation modified.
5. *Ibid.*, p. 214, translation modified.

1923 and the end of hopes for world revolution played an important role in the elimination of Trotsky, who demanded that the Party play the card of world revolution. Likewise, during the subsequent Bukharin-Stalin politics until 1929, a decisive role in the abandonment of that political line was played by the events related in *Man's Fate* [*La Condition Humaine*] such as the Chiang Kai-Shek democrats' break with the Party, and by the politics which democrats pursued in the West. The phenomenon of Trotsky's elimination cannot be analyzed merely at the individual level.

Again at the sociological level, one of the best known studies of administration maintains that there are conservative and innovative tendencies in French administration, describes them rather precisely, and poses the question of which will gain the upper hand. This research situates itself outside any functionality and is satisfied precisely to describe that administration. In 1966, however, after the inquiry had been going on for a long time, we find the following note in a journal: "To progress in comprehending change in the midst of administrative organizations it seems necessary to depart from the framework of those organizations themselves. [This effort to connect intra-administrative transformations and transformations of the environment in the same analysis forms precisely the object of our second program of reaearch.]"[6] It has taken years to inquire into the functionality of the phenomenon under study! Thus—and I still do not know what has been done since—the concept of functionality in relation to a collective subject appears very late or is completely eliminated.

Moving now to the literary level, where the domain of my research is situated, imagine for a moment that Racine had been educated not at Port-Royal but instead, as could have happened, by the Jesuits. Given Racine's genius, it is not impossible that he would nonetheless have written plays of genius. They certainly would not have been the same ones. There is no necessary link between the individual Racine and the plays he wrote: thousands of accidents influenced and determined their structure and detail. If instead we place ourselves in the perspective of the collective subject and, in questions of culture, of the social group oriented toward the overall organization of human relations—that is, the perspective of social classes—then perhaps Port-Royal could not

---

6. Pierre Grémion, "Résistance au changement des administrations territoriales: le cas des institutions régionales" in *Sociologie du Travail*, no. 3, 1965, p. 295[n].

produce theater of genius, but it certainly could not have produced lyric hymns or Molière's plays, because the structure of its thinking was such that everything emanating from it necessarily had to have the structure of tragedy. And at that level the details which can never be accounted for at the level of individual psychology become strictly necessary.

For example, the question of why Don Juan marries every month—which goes against the verisimilitude demanded in the 17th century—will be difficult to explain in relation to Molière. But if we admit that *Don Juan* is written in the perspective of the court nobility and that in it Molière takes a position against the court nobles themselves (and not against the bourgeois as in *The Bourgeois Gentleman* and *The Miser*, or against the Jansenists as in *The Misanthrope*, or against the members of the Société du Saint-Sacrament as in *Tartuffe*), then we understand that in *Don Juan* he could have only isolated scenes and no action, and that Molière's constant attitude is, "What Don Juan does is right, but he exaggerates; he gives alms to the poor, but he asks them to blaspheme," and so forth: that is the play's whole structure. But tradition gives Molière a Don Juan who has a series of mistresses. The answer to the question must thus conform to the play's structure: it must pose the problem at the level of libertinism, within the court nobility's exaggerations. Then the answer is concise: one cannot say, "You have mistresses monthly; you must have them every three months": in fact, the rigorous structuration is, "You marry, which is right; but you marry peasants. A noble does not marry peasants; and you marry every month, which is too often." This was the play's structuration, which demanded that everything Don Juan does be correct but exaggerated except in the one domain where there is no exaggeration, in courage: Don Juan is extremely courageous, and there he is beyond reproach.

Likewise there is the example of Hector, the dead man who speaks in *Andromaque*: especially for the 17th century, this is absolutely improbable, and Racine did not like improbabilities. Whenever he introduces them it is for reasons of coherence. In the Jansenist perspective there was no escape from the world; the figures who corrspond to God, but are not God, keep silent. Inversely, when a solution is presented in the world—when Andromaque discovers she can wed Pyrrhus to save Astyanax and then commit suicide to resolve the contradiction—then Hector speaks: despite the improbability, God speaks.

Examples could just as well be taken from contemporary plays. When in *The Blacks* Genet addresses the problem of the opposition between Blacks and Whites, he cannot have the white characters played by Whites for a very specific reason: the radical conflict between Blacks and Whites cannot be related in a spectacle where black and white actors collaborate. This has consequences for the entire play: if Blacks play the white actors, they must participate in the ceremony, the ritual. The reality which was on stage in the other plays is outside it this time. In this perspective one can even account for the order of the cues in the play. Results on this level can be obtained working from the collective subject.

To know what Jean or Pierre thinks, what their behavior is when they lift a table, and how they see it, it must be taken into account that they are *together* to lift it: and everything which is history occurs in this perspective. If we admit the perspective of the collective subject, the first thing we can dispense with is the concept of the transcendental subject, one of the most painful crosses in the history of philosophy. How did this concept arise? It arose at the moment in the history of philosophy when philosophers understood that man participates in creating the world. They were still working with the individual, empirical subject; but clearly the empirical self, rather than creating the world (whence came the idea of a transcendental subject whose consciousness created the world), instead finds the world before him. But if we put ourselves at the level of the transindividual subject, then it—social groups—has really created the roads, houses, institutions, and social relations as well as the mental categories with which we comprehend them; and we no longer need a transcendental subject. The idea of the creation of society, social institutions, moral laws, and mental categories is effectively placed at the level of the empirical subject; thus we can work on the level of positive science. On this basis all the dualities dominating contemporary philosophy—those on the level of the individual subject, which gives rise to idealism, or those on the level of the negation of the subject, which is the final consequence of any mechanical materialism—disappear, making way for operative dualities which, however, are not radical in character.

I have already mentioned the subject-object duality. But from this perspective it must be taken into account that concepts like metalanguage are useful and necessary providing they are not made absolute. If I speak about French in French, or if I speak about language, I am not in a radical metalanguage. It must be taken into account that I am speaking about the French language in French—that I am speaking about the French language and that the concept of metalanguage is operative provided no radical opposition is made between language and metalanguage.

Likewise for judgments of fact and value. If judgments of fact are structured by an ensemble of mental categories linked to the *praxis* of groups, then value judgments basically ground judgments of fact in a group's perspective. And of course those judgments of fact determine *praxis* and ground value judgments. To study the history of political behavior I must begin with the social reality where it developed; but to comprehend social facts I must take into consideration the value judgments with whose help men have constructed them. A structuralist article opposing me published in an English journal[7] begins by saying: Goldmann sociologically analyzes the different ideas of Marxism, whose action he negates; and further on: he speaks of action, whose historical conditioning he forgets. But of course both are present; and precisely, to affirm the one does not negate the other. The question is no longer to affirm that the two elements are present, but to know in each specific case what the type of relation is and how functionality is realized. As an individual confronting the world, things are there and I can only judge them: there is this house, and then there is the fact that it does or does not please me or that it is beautiful or ugly. But on the level of the collective subject, things are in transformation and are linked to the subject's behavior; and facts cannot be radically separated from it—from their valorization.

Likewise for continuity and discontinuity. If I buy a car I can say that there is a discontinuity between, for example, the Citroën DS and the 3CV which followed it; but in the perspective of the social group, of the auto industry and Citroën, there is a continuity, a continuous evolution which creates the discontinuity at a certain moment. In philosophy this was traditionally called the passage from quantity to quality. Social groups are transformed within given structures and at a certain moment the transition is made from one structure to the other. It is altogether absurd to imagine discontinuity without transformation, in the manner of all linguistic structualists (Althusser recognizes the problem but thinks

7. Miriam Glucksmann, "Lucien Goldmann: Humanist or Marxist?" in *New Left Review* 56 (July-August 1969) [*Trans.*].

it cannot be resolved for the time being). Thus the fundamental problem is to understand that any discontinuity presupposes transformations within a given structure; and inversely that continuity, becoming, entails discontinuities—and that this is always a relative problem.

Likewise for explication and comprehension, the object of so many academic discussions, in which comprehension is so often assimilated to empathy, sympathy, and so forth. To comprehend a phenomenon is to describe its structure and to isolate its meaning. To explicate a phenomenon is to explain its genesis on the basis of a developing functionality which begins with a subject. And there is no radical difference between comprehension and explication. To explicate one of Pascal's *Pensées*, I must refer to all of them; and if I study them all I comprehend them. But their genesis must be explicated, so I appeal to Jansenism; I can comprehend Jansenism by appealing to the *noblesse de robe*; and so forth. Research is always situated at the two levels of structure and functionality. Functionality implies the subject; and at the historical level, the collective subject is the only subject which can account for the ensemble of phenomena, when we are dealing with texts known in their entirety.

Examining all the other dualities I have mentioned would require a long development. I want to end this paper by stressing an idea which seems especially important: one side of the facts must necessarily be eliminated in the position of the individual subject, or of facts which exist outside value judgments and outside the collective subjects which created them (the line from Descartes to Sartre), as well as by the much more radical line from Holbach to contemporary structuralism or linguistics (the first does not see structure; the second does not see the subject which creates genesis, becoming, and functionality). Thus they end up deforming the facts and becoming ideological. One of the most important concerns of contemporary academic reform, however, is manifest in the requirement of multidisciplinarity. This is good and useful, since there are continual linkages not only within the reality of the cosmos but also, and especially, in social reality, among different sectors. A literary phenomenon cannot be understood outside painting, economics, linguistics, and so forth. But it should be understood once and for all that it is not a matter of combining the positive research of a sector which does not take the subject into consideration, with the idealist studies starting from the individual or psychological subject which do not take social reality into account. This forgets the intimate relation between functionality and structure—that is, it is not dialectical. This supposed creation of interdisciplinarity with three or four unilateral perspectives does not create a scientific perspective. Interdisciplinarity will arise implicitly insofar as the problem is formulated in each discipline, insofar as sociologists take into account that a sociology must not be positivistic but must take the transindividual subject into consideration as an actor transforming reality, and insofar as all the different sectors of the human sciences become dialectical. Then, of course, there will be specializations and specialists in the framework of this interdisciplinarity. Dialectical thinkers have not waited for this situation. While I have had a chair in the sociology of literature for a long time, sociologists generally missed the literary fact when they studied literature, because they were looking in it for the reflection of collective consciousness rather than for the creation of structures, and because students of literature considered sociology as mere external conditioning.

The relations among sociology and psychology, law and sociology, and ultimately all sectors of the human sciences can become truly interdisciplinary only by reintroducing the creative subject at the interior of social life: human groups, collectivities, and above all, in the historical dimension, social classes. An authentic interdisciplinarity presupposes dialectical human sciences; any regrouping of positivist or idealist perspectives will create not an interdisciplinarity, but only some administrative organizations in which the different sectors will wear a single hat yet will remain partial nonetheless.

6. THE DIALECTIC TODAY*

I want to refer my paper on the dialectic today to two earlier discussions: yesterday's, and another one here last year in which I was an active participant. Beginning with these two discussions, what I want to propose today is not at all the result of research or of a theory: I will venture only to raise questions and to suggest first elements of a research hypothesis which might constitute the basis for the beginnings of later positive research. But all the same, there is the intial problem of knowing how to formulate the questions and what are the first steps toward the answer.

I want to refer first to the discussion following Holtz's lecture about the actualization of past philosophies and of Hegel and, secondly, to the problem of bureaucracy. Holtz correctly explained that it is necessary not to read philosophers simply as surpassed historical facts which are studied to know what happened a hundred or a thousand years ago, but instead to actualize them. I replied that I agreed, but that the fundamental problem was knowing how to accomplish that actualization. It seems a bad actualization to say that all of Marxism and all our problems were already in Hegel, or to say that Hegel holds no interest and that our problems are essentially different. Actualizing a philosopher or a

---

*This essay was read at the Korçula (Yugoslavia) Summer School at the end of August, 1970. It has been published in *L'homme et la Société*, no. 19, January-March 1971.

philosophical thought presupposes comprehending it as it was, with its different positive elements, its internal coherence, and its development within a social reality: beginning there, we can see how certain elements can still respond to our problems.

But specifically regarding Hegel, there is an actualization which seems to me a principal one for the history of philosophy: this is what is most significant in Georg Lukács' second period. You know that much as I admire Lukács up to 1925, there are many points on which I disagree with and have formulated my reservations about the post-1936 Lukács. Nonetheless, he had an idea—which arose from the problematic of Stalinism—which has allowed us to see much more clearly not what could have been—what could have been done with German philosophy and the dialectic—but what actually was done, and how it arose in Europe. In fact, it was from a present problematic that Lukács was able to see that European dialectical philosophy, the dialectic, and classical German literature—especially Hegel and Goethe—arose from the problem of the Jacobin and Napoleonic dictatorships: that it was a question which faces us but which earlier faced the democratic thinkers of that age. They are for freedom; but freedom began to be asserted through the Jacobin dictatorship, and subsequently through the Napoleonic dictatorship which referred to freedom and the Revolution less and less or even not at all, but which was objectively opposed to the Ancien Régime since it was founded on the distribution of land and rested on the peasants. Thinkers like Hegel and Goethe had to discuss the problem, address it, and seek an integration of which rationalism was no longer capable. Seeing how Madame de Staël addresses the same problem, and categorically refuses to imagine that evil might be the road to good, suffices to show that *Faust* was the decisive step. For the first time, it expressed the fact that the pact with the devil is the road to heaven, that it is not only the road but *the only* road, that nature changes, and that things are not eternally good or bad but must be judged in context. And this suffices to show that all the great categories of Hegelian dialectical thought arose not out of a pure philosophical speculation—Hegel's consciousness of this may have been less clear—but instead out of the discussion of problems which are ours today and which were Lukács' when he tried—not directly but through an aesthetic approach—to analyze the political problems of his time and Stalinism. This is a Hegelian actualization.

There have since been other Hegelian actualizations in France; of course we can discuss whether or not they are valuable. The right Hegelianism of Kojève and Weil showed how, after Napoleon's fall and the end of the French Revolution, Hegel was faced with a problematic rather similar or in some respects rather akin to the one facing us. History continued; the dialectical position which I will discuss always required not the opposition of moral values to history but an inquiry, within historical reality, as to how one could insert oneself in it. The result has been an entirely different appreciation of the Prussian State, which to Hegel—and such is the theory of our right Hegelians—appeared to be relatively the most progressive factor. In France, this gave rise to articles and studies which in the name of Hegel, analyzing his reaction, began with the idea that history is made by bureaucrats, men of State, or chiefs of State. Thus—there is even a rather characteristic article by Weil—arose a defense of Stalin against the Trotskyist reprobates, and of Western governments against the Christian reprobates who tried to introduce moral values—whereas it is men of State who make history. That whole discussion is also an actualization; and I do not think that Lukács and right Hegelianism are so far wrong. *The Phenomenology of Mind* is one thing and *The Philosophy of Right* is another: one was written before the 1789 Revolution and the other afterward; and therefore Hegel had to formulate the problems at different levels. This actualization of course poses all the problems of scientific research; but it tries to see what a philosophy actually was in its time. Hence it leads us to ask, in situations which certainly have common elements or in others which do not, how and to what extent we can answer as the philosophers did, or differently.

Concerning the same discussion I also want to say a few words about the problem of bureaucracy. I replied to Holtz that I believe there is a scientific error or insufficiency whose practical consequence is always to talk about "bureaucracy," "capitalism," or "socialism" out of relation to specific studies, as though one were dealing historically with a single phenomenon, and to omit the fact that there are very different bureaucracies with very different functions. Thus, whereas Marx could very well use the term "capitalism" since in his time there was only a single type of capitalism (liberal capitalism), the term was no longer sufficient even for Lenin and Rosa Luxemburg, who had to talk about imperialist capitalism. And since the second and third phases of capitalism are both imperialist, we now need three different terms:

the term "imperialist" has become insufficient to characterize the third phase, and a theoretical term must distinguish specific traits. Following the capitalism between the two World Wars, which was rocked by crises because the mechanisms of market regulation had disappeared, today we have technocratic, organizational capitalism: but since both are imperialist we need different terms to distinguish them. Holtz replied that he agreed on the need for a general term on the one hand, and for concrete studies of each case on the other. Everyone who has constructed a general theory recognizes, of course, the need to concretize it in each analysis; it even forms part of the general theory to say that there is the common category of bureaucracy or capitalism, and then the analysis of each concrete historical case. But that is precisely what does not seem scientific. The level of scientific research is located between the two: between pure historical analysis of the localized case and the general theory which eclipses the difference. Scientific analysis presupposes a schematization or typology, and one of the most important tasks is to establish the level at which that typology is operative. Everyone agrees that if we construct a very general theory of capitalism we must then analyze French, Italian, German, and English capitalism in this or that period. But what is essential is to situate the analysis at the three levels of liberal capitalism, capitalism in crisis, and organizational capitalism— which is neither the concrete analysis of any particular case which grounds it nor the very general concept which is no longer operative at some moment. The level of schematizations, moreover, is not permanent or eternal. As history continues, the researcher must always ask where the operative level of analysis is situated; if he is mistaken, corrections can arise only from free discussion of the objections.

Today, the essential problematic is to know where the operative level of an analysis of bureaucracy is situated. Of course, a general theory of bureaucracy is always completed by the analysis of the Polish or Hungarian bureaucracy at this or that time. But what interests me is that this double level is precisely nonscientific, and that the scientific level is that at which a typology is attempted. I will propose a typology which may be bad since it is not based on long research; but despite everything I think it can constitute a starting point.

I have entitled this paper "The Dialectic Today" because in fact I think that a whole series of the fundamental categories of dialectical thought, which Lukács has shown to have arisen from the need to integrate the problems of the Jacobin and Napoleonic dictatorships into the problematic of a philosophy of history oriented toward freedom, remain valid for our thinking and our problematic. I will try to list these categories, and then to move on to their concrete application.

The first, principal idea of dialectical thought is the category of totality. This is no accident: a dialectician cannot do the history of ideas outside the history of society: as Hegel, I think, or Lukács said, the history of the problem is the problem of history; or, the history of ideas forms part of the history of facts. Totality is the idea that a phenomenon can be comprehended only by first inserting it in the broader structure of which it is part and in which it has a function, the latter being its objective meaning independently of whether or not the men acting and creating it are conscious of it. It is the category of meaningful structure, which can be comprehended only by inserting it in a broader meaningful structure and in the whole of history.

The second great Hegelian category, which is not at all mysterious or speculative, is that of the identity of subject and object: according to me it is partial; according to Hegel it is total. It asserts simply that if humanity is historical, if the subjects of action, creation, and praxis are social groups (Marx specifies them as social classes), if social groups are collective subjects, then all thought about history and society is science and consciousness; and the group which is thinking is the subject and object of thought. If for example Marxism is the thought of the proletariat—this could be disputed—then *Capital* is a thought of the proletariat about the proletariat, since the proletariat analyzing capitalist society analyzes itself as part of that capitalist society. But in analyzing itself it is no longer the same, since, especially with the dissemination and influence of *Capital* and Marxist thought, it gains a self-consciousness other than that which preceded the development of Marxism. Hence the idea arises that theories, judgments of fact, can be founded only on value judgments, and that value judgments can be founded only on judgments of fact; that they cannot be separated nor can subject and object be separated. This is the radical critique of all positivism (and positivism is not merely a small school, but includes any claim of a radical rupture between judgments of fact and value judgments).

These Hegelian categories are all recovered in Marxism; and it is no accident that they were reactualized in Europe around, say, the years 1917-1923: first by Lenin in the *Philosophical Notebooks*, secondly by Lukács in *History and Class Consciousness*, and thirdly, I believe, somewhat later in Gramsci's concretely philosophical analyses. Furthermore, it is not accidental that in the interim, with Mehring, Plekhanov, Kautsky, Bernstein, and even Lenin at the time he wrote *Materialism and Empiriocriticism*, Marxism was just as positivistic as academic science. It is not accidental because the problems from which the dialectic arose—revolution and its strategy and tactics (in the French Revolution)—were actualized again around 1917. Insofar as they addressed these problem, and despite the very strong positivist tradition, Marxist thinkers were obliged to return to the dialectical problematic, even if only to a certain extent because the givens of a dialectical sociological analysis were not yet sufficient. And if after 1923 this renaissance of dialectical thought subsequently ended, it was because the revolutionary period was clearly over: we know that with the 1923 defeat in Germany, after 1925-1926, there was no longer a trace of any of this.

Because the attempt to Heideggerianize Marxism is often made, I add parenthetically that Heidegger, who came out of Lask and the same milieu in which Lukácsian thought developed, of course understood these issues perfectly well. It was then not a central, but an important element of what was discussed at Freiburg and Heidelberg. Perhaps Heidegger's importance was to create a language and then give a reactionary theory of the elements Lukács had developed. But there is an extraordinary kinship between the Heideggerian *Sein* and the Lukácsian totality, between the Heideggerian being-for-death and authenticity and Lukacs' analysis of the consciousness of limits in "Metaphysik der Tragödie," between the *"Zuhandenheit"* and *"Vorhandenheit"* described by Heidegger and the praxis Lukács opposes to objective presence, and between Heidegger's traditional ontology and the perception of *Sein* and Lukács' distinction between traditional and dialectical philosophy. Thus, to Heideggerianize Marxism can only be to recover in the language of a reactionary philosophy categories already translated from a Marxist analysis into a Heideggerian, existentialist analysis. It can also be added that at the beginning of the analysis in *Being and Time* and on its last page,[1] there are direct polemical references indicating against whom the book is

---

1. *Being and Time*, trans. John Macquarrie and Edward Robinson (New York: Harper & Row, 1962), pp. 72, 487 [*Trans.*].

written and in relation to whom every page is written: the theoretician of the *"Verdinglichkeit des Bewusstseins,"* in quotation marks, the theoretician of the reification of consciousness—half of Lukács' *History and Class Consciousness* was devoted to the *Verdinglichkeit des Bewusstseins.*

But what is important is that dialectical thought has always been linked to the problem of social transformation, of revolution: that it arose in the French Revolution, was reactualized with Marx at the time of the 1848 Revolution, and was reactualized and reappeared in Marxist thought when analogous problems occurred around 1917 and immediately thereafter.

Now I want to refer to two analyses: one which I have developed twice and which, it seems to me, should not be abandoned but specified; and another concerning the sociology of bureaucracy and its functionality.

The former has continued for years, and perhaps I let myself be too influenced by the theoreticians of that time and also by a reality which was still not fully developed and took on its concrete forms only after June 1968. I saw the problematic of modern society pretty much as follows. On the one hand, there were theoreticians who claimed that technocratic society was perfectly equilibrated, had resolved all problems, was raising the standard of living, etc. These theoreticians had very different political connotations. For some, this stabilization of technocratic society was on a par with the disappearance of all spirit of contestation, to the benefit of everyone's adaptation: this was the end of ideologies for Daniel Bell and Raymond Aron, who saw it as a positive phenomenon, as the onset of the ideal world. With a certain melancholy, David Riesman declared that it was the disappearance of internal radar. Finally, for Herbert Marcuse it was the apocalypse, the reign of one-dimensional man, where organizational capitalism increasingly suppressed the creative dimension, the critical dimension, and left man only the adaptive dimension. Through entirely different judgments, these three groups of theoreticians agreed that organizational capitalism had settled in, if not for eternity, at least for a long time: it brought a rise in production, in well-being, and so forth. In opposition were the theoreticians of the new working class, rallying to the Yugoslav idea of self-management: first Trentin and Foa in Italy; then, introducing their ideas into French sociology, Serge Mallet and André Gorz. They explained, and I think correctly, that new factors of contestation different from the old ones were developing: the new salaried middle classes, the "new working class"—basically, the skilled workers, technicians, the salaried middle strata arising in society. I acknowledge that I developed my own analysis from that angle. Both things are possible: a technocratic society can be imagined among groups which in any case are well paid if the development of their consciousness is suppressed; but there are powerful reasons for admitting that these groups acquire consciousness of their situation, that an evolution toward socialism is occurring, and that it is a problem of struggling for consciousness.

Today I would call this analysis not false but schematic and unilateral. The evolution of the last two years indicates traits about which I can formulate only hypotheses, but which are conspicuous and demand reflection. The first new fact seems to be that elements are appearing in contemporary European capitalist society which can seriously persuade one that the technocratic strata themselves will be oriented toward self-management. Minority ruling strata have always needed social bases; until now those bases were precisely the autonomous petty bourgeoisie or the peasants who are presently disappearing. Thus the problem of finding other social bases will necessarily arise for the rulers of technocratic society. These other bases can only be the new middle strata; at least, say, the upper end of the new working class or salaried middle strata which technocratic society is developing. But just as concessions had to be made to the workers in order to integrate them, and just as concessions had to be made to the traditional petty bourgeoisie in the liberal world, concessions will also have to be made to these strata (although the attempt will be made to limit them). But mere concessions of income will not suffice for the simple reason that the more income rises, the less a rise in income is decisive. In one way or another, the evolution on the side of the dominant classes will probably go in the direction of a compromise permitting orientation toward certain structural reforms involving participation, toward collaboration and structural reforms in businesses rather than toward true self-management. Some bourgeoisies will resist and will remain behind: all countries will not remain at the same level. Reforms will occur and the countries adopting them will forge ahead, or else they will not occur and the countries will remain behind: it is a fact we can depend on.

This second important idea means that this historical evolution, which seems to me the fundamental trait of modern society and of its transformations, will be able to follow different paths insofar as what develops in any case is an internal transformation in which a class will progressively gain influence and power in the existing technocratic society. Very schematically, this evolution occurs in the bourgeoisie's mode of development in the midst of feudal society, beginning with economic and social transformations before succeeding in political transformation. The experience of the bourgeois revolution has shown that this evolution can occur in different ways—schematically, in the French way or the German way: in the revolutionary way with the people's participation and the structuration of an essentially different society; or through minimal reforms compelled from above. The societies born in these ways are entirely different, which is one of modern society's great problems. If we are dialectical and try to ask what the subject of the transformation is—not arbitrarily how it has to be, but what the real subject of the transformation is—then I believe we must turn toward this new salaried middle stratum, this new working class. But because the roads are different we also have to ask what the possible roads are; and these different possible roads admit of different, although not unequivocally different, results. If we draw up the balance sheet of the revolutionary road by which the bourgeoisie took power in France and its reformist road to power in Germany, in France we have on the one hand a society where the Jacobin, democratic revolutionary traditions have indisputably influenced all of French culture. But on the other hand, this same bourgeoisie which had been obliged to appeal to the people to support it in the Revolution, afterwards had to rid itself of the people; and in France we have had two of the most violent repressions to eliminate the proletariat from the society to whose creation it had contributed: June 1848 and the Paris Commune. That is—and this is extremely important—the problematic now facing us is to know what forces, as historical forces beginning to be manifest, can actually have a decisive influence on the way this transformation will occur: not in their program or in their analysis of the revolutionary situation, but in reality (I think these forces began to be expressed in events like those of the left in 1968). On the role of these forces—not merely on the individuals, of course, but on the social strata behind them—will probably depend the problematic of knowing whether this new society, which is to be oriented toward self-management and, to use the decisive term, toward economic democracy, will be humanistic and will include important elements of what can be called socialism, or will simply secure the participation of a very small elitist group through entirely conservative, prosaic compromises. Precisely insofar as transformations occur in the way which is most democratic and most valid in its hopes of human and humanistic cultural creation, we must also take into account the grave danger that someday the technocrats, the technicians, and even the producers might try to rid themselves of the popular strata, as the bourgeoisie rid itself of the people. I do not know if it will be possible or will be achieved, but the essential function of aware socialist thinkers is precisely to do everything possible on the one hand to assure the most democratic, humanistic evolution possible, and on the other to prevent the recurrence of reactions such as June 1848 and, above all, the Commune. Thus, I believe the new working class theorists' analysis has to be modified here and in this respect.

What are the real forces now which can act in the direction of a transformation toward, say, the French rather than the German path: toward a more democratic, popular, humanistic path more imbued with socialist thought, intention, and orientation? First of all, there are precisely the old strata, which must not be neglected: the traditional proletariat, even the petty bourgeoisie which was privileged until now—all the strata hard hit by current social transformations. Equally, there is a fundamental stratum whose sociology, however, remains to be done: the university. I will not repeat what I published last year in *Praxis*;[2] but for structural reasons the university is a social stratum which cannot easily be integrated into the new technocratic society on the path of transformation without orienting itself toward a profound self-management. There are, of course, the national minorities such as Blacks in America. And there are also the most radicalized strata of the new working class, and many intellectuals. But above all I want to add a new stratum which, if not necessarily produced by technocratic society, in any case seems to be one of the possible dangers it gives rise to: the enormous stratum of "paupers" developing in American cities. The extraordinary pauperization in New York or Chicago clearly represents an important social problematic. All these strata can be and are being radicalized. In any case they can intervene in the transformation process: old strata which exist only for a time and will be absorbed if the

---

2. "Pouvoir et humanisme" in *Praxis*, vol. 6, nos. 1-2, 1970, pp. 24-44; republished in Lucien Goldmann, *Marxisme et sciences humaines* (Paris: Gallimard, Idées, 1970), pp. 327-361 [*Trans*].

transformation occurs, and new strata like students, certain fractions of the new working class, and the "paupers" which technocratic society produces at least in certain conditions and perhaps necessarily. These are the strata which have a function and determine the modalities of the road to be chosen. But it must not be forgotten that even if the extreme leftists [*gauchistes*], the crises of the student movement, and the 1968 crises in France are the first manifestations of this phenomenon, it would be false to see in them the possibility or even the dawning moment of a revolution of the old kind: the socialist revolution of the proletariat. In fact, I believe that these events will have a decisive orientation and can be a decisive factor in society's evolution, and that if we are socialists we must perceive all that they can bring to the socialist character of this evolution or transformation. But I believe we must also understand that our role is precisely to consolidate that socialist orientation and to prevent future conflicts which might be analogous to those between the bourgeoisie and the proletariat.

On this basis I now want to approach the problem of bureaucracy and to propose a schematization of the concept of bureaucratic structure, for whatever it is worth. In a year I may find it poor and modify it, but I submit it for discussion. I have indicated why I do not believe the concept of bureaucracy, like the general concept of socialism or capitalism, is operative. On the contrary, up to the present there have been very different types of bureaucracies which have fulfilled different functions; and I offer a schematic, proposed typology which might serve as a basis for reflection.

First, analyzed largely in a valid way, I believe, by Max Weber, there was a bureaucratic structure which was linked to liberal capitalism and which allowed it to develop. It developed as liberal State bureaucracy and has very little to do with the Stalinist bureaucracy, for example, or with other types. What is important is that in this liberal society the working class had a particular position which was not that of the structure of the revolutionary class which could negate that society. We know that in the West this class has been integrated to a large extent, and that there has never been a proletarian revolution. But this class escaped reification, as Marx saw quite well independently of this integration, which he did not take into account but which has occurred. Insofar as this class escaped reification, however, it was not culturally integrable as a class. It has been integrated politically and economically, but on that basis it has created a counterculture which on the cultural plane is radically opposed to the dominant culture.

This has been precisely the function of parties with revolutionary ideology: beginning with the traditional social-democratic parties, they represented a sort of society within society. They gave way to a second form of bureaucracy which was functional and which, for reasons I cannot clarify here, had to develop. Moreover, whereas they were actually reformist and integrated, these bureaucracies had a false revolutionary consciousness. But they also developed in a very specific oppositional atmosphere (Bebel was very proud of never having shake a minister's hand) and with an attitude of democracy within the movement (perhaps Rosa Luxemburg could never take power, but she could express herself freely within the movement). The counterculture grounded in freedom and socialism was essential. This meant that the working class, which as it knew was to a great extent integrated on the economic and social planes, but which was not integrated on the plane of consciousness and had created a counterculture, was itself never able to create the revolutionary movement. But on the contrary, every time a social crisis occurred it was able to play a revolutionary role, the role of an important oppositional force. We must also account for the fact that there was no revolution in the West except for the role of the Spanish proletariat, the French proletariat in the Popular Front and the 1968 strike, etc. The proletariat's potential for revolutionary explosion and for a revolutionary but periodic function, which will last as long as the proletariat does, was based simply on the fact that, though economically and socially integrated, it nonetheless possessed a counterculture which at certain times could become revolutionary. This has produced the very specific bureaucracy of the social-democratic parties.[3]

---

3. [Denoël editor's note] At the time of his paper at Korçula, Goldmann had not had time to develop his thinking on this point; it seems useful to specify it by quoting a passage which returns to this problem from the introduction to his last book, *Marxisme et sciences humaines*, written in September, 1970, shortly before his death: "Where the traditional working class is concerned, even if it is true that in Western societies it has been integrated into the capitalist order and has never played the role Marxian analyses attributed to it, it remains no less true that this integration has had a specific character unlike the integration of any other social class. From social democracy, and especially German social democracy before the war, to the contemporary Communist parties, it was carried out on the epistemological and cultural plane in the form of an authentic and strongly oppositional counterculture. This was manifested in the creation of politically integrated workers' parties, which were reformist and conservative but culturally and ideologically oppositional and contesting.

"Consequently, although of itself it never launched a revolutionary crisis, from June

A third type of bureaucracy arose in Russia, where a non-proletarian revolutionary party was involved. (The great opposition between Lenin and Luxemburg is this: although Lenin's conclusions were entirely different, like Bernstein he knew that the proletariat is not a fundamentally revolutionary force but can be integrated and can play a role. A reading of *What Is to Be Done?* suffices to show the elements common to Lenin and Bernstein.) The party's function was to unite all the discontented, the peasants, the national minorities, and the proletarians, and to organize a revolutionary structure with which to take power. And after the seizure of power, a very different type of bureaucracy arose in it. For those who were still revolutionaries and socialists, this bureaucracy had to have the tactical function of organizing combat, which, of course, sometimes tactically required bureaucratic functions which were very questionable but were conceived and regarded as means of realizing the revolution.

Afterward comes a fourth form of bureaucracy, Stalinism, whose bases must be accurately perceived: the check of revolution in the West (Germany), then the break with Chaing Kai-shek, the elimination of the left opposition (Trotsky), and the elimination of the right (Bukharin). Stalinism is not at all the history of one man or of a personal power; it is not an excrescence. In a predominantly peasant nation which must defend itself against an extremely powerful encirclement—as Trotsky said, moreover, styling it as

---

1848 to May 1968 the working class nonetheless actively intervened as an oppositional, contesting force every time such a crisis arose from external circumstances—except when all action was successfully blocked by its organizations' immediate interests, as in 1914 in Germany in relation to the Empire's strategic interests or in 1933 and 1939 in relation to the USSR's external political interests.

"The specific character of this integration and its particularly important consequences must, of course, be analyzed and grounded on the theoretical level. I want to formulate a hypothesis on this point: integration seems to result not only from the amelioration of the standard of living and from a certain number of trade union victories, but also from active, everyday participation in the process of production and, implicitly, in the functioning of capitalist society. The culturally and ideologically contesting, oppositional character of this integration seems explainable—and here Marx's inspired analysis is still entirely valid—by the fact that workers having nothing to sell but their labor power—which means, ultimately, themselves—must necessarily, although to varying degrees, remain rebels against reification, against adaptation to the market, and against the transformation of goods into commodities. In other words: integration founded on participation in production, on material advantages, and on trade union victories; tendency toward an existential refusal of generalized quantification on the market and of the transformation of goods and men into commodities characterized primarily or even solely by their price" (pp. 8-10).

Bonapartism—it is a politics which decides not to enter into external conflict and to oppose any revolution in the capitalist countries, since revolution alarms the bourgeoisie and creates counterrevolutionary unity.

The key to Stalinist bureaucratization is precisely that it is a bureaucracy which, so as to be able to maintain its influence on the Western proletariat which is in the same situation, for the first time defends the counterculture and the revolutionary position. But at the same time, for very specific reasons involving Russia, it must oppose any revolutionary movement which would threaten to create bourgeois unity against the Soviet Union.

Here a type of bureaucracy arises with a very different hardness, a different cynicism. It has a specific function and cannot be confused with Leninist or social-democratic bureaucracy, or with that of liberal societies. It is an extremely specific phenomenon, which requires sociological analysis. We must ask not only why this bureaucracy arose in Russia, but also whether it preserved its revolutionary ideology and its countercultural aspect. It was a question of maintaining influence precisely on a Western proletariat which was not being integrated into bourgeois culture but whose attitude corresponded precisely to what the Stalinist bureaucracy's orientation then desired: preserving a counter-cultural consciousness without provoking revolutionary crisis. This explains the influence Stalinism has been able to maintain over the Western proletariat.

Finally, we should be aware of a new but fundamental phenomenon: the birth out of technological transformations of something very different, which is unlike any of the four old forms of bureaucracy: technocracy. This is the direction of a society which tends to organize itself rationally; here again, it conflicts with traditional bureaucracies which are certainly very powerful, probably having economic consequences in Russia and the socialist world as well. Technocratization is more advanced in the West, but the problem is arising everywhere and it is important to be aware of it.

I propose this analysis as a beginning; it may be a bad one. But it is absolutely essential that we create a *localized historical typology* of the different phases in the history of the workers' movement, of the corresponding bureaucracies, and of the present situation of bureaucracy. This must be done by analysis at the level of the central force and the tendencies in the evolution toward economic democracy which can be realized by collaboration, by compromise, or even by the path of revolutionary conflict. Also we must analyze the modifications in this path which can be introduced by factors other than the most conservative strata of technocracy and the new working class, by the strata more attached to socialism, and by every social phenomenon which can be understood in the present crisis.

We must neither plunge into illusion, believing that we are in a revolutionary situation, nor believe that we are not and that these forces of contestation represent nothing. Instead, we must arrive at a real sociological analysis showing the possibilities all this holds, the roads the evolution may take, and the risks it includes, so that we can ask what position should be assumed by socialist thinkers trying to orient the transformations in which society finds itself today. The dialectic's great value lies precisely not in judging morally—not in saying merely that we want democracy and it must be introduced, or that we want revolution and it must necessarily be made—but in asking what the real forces of transformation are and how the subject of the transformation can be found in reality, in the object, in society, so that we can attempt to speak in its perspective and, knowing the risk of defeat full well, to assure the road toward socialism.

A BRIEF TRIBUTE TO GOLDMANN*

Lucien Goldmann came to be a very dear friend of mine, for whom I had the most lively admiration. Of course, this admiration pertained to his rare intellectual qualities: his dynamism, which never allowed him to rest and drove him from problem to problem, to endeavors which succeeded one another endlessly, as if each of them, scarcely undertaken, was already pregnant with sequels; his inventiveness, which enabled him to renew questions, as he succeeded in doing radically with the subject of Jansenism and the theater of Racine; the precision of his deductions, which enabled him to invent the Abbey Barcos by a sort of calculus recalling, as others before me have noticed, Verrier's deductions in discovering Neptune (and the achievement is unique in sociology..); the delicacy of his analyses, permitting him to perceive what no one had seen in a novel or play to the point that his reader is taken with uneasiness · before being reassured by the coherence of the total analysis; his professional conscientiousness, which obliged him not only to go back to the sources, but also to undertake that uncommon practice of exploring all the sources; his ever-alert curiosity, which never wandered and which was accompanied by an exceptional aptitude for passing from the concrete to the general idea. In brief, I cannot enumerate all the particular qualities which made Goldmann a complete researcher and a creator of ideas such as one rarely finds in a lifetime.

But besides his intelligence, what always struck me about

---

*The three following pieces are taken from *Hommage a Lucien Goldmann*, a special issue of *Revue de l'Institut de sociologie de l'Universite Libre de Bruxelles*, 3/4 (1973), pp. 525-547. The first and third appendices have been translated by Ileana Rodriguez and Marc Zimmerman. The Adorno-Goldmann exchange originally took place at the second international colloquium on the sociology of literature at Royaumont. (For further details, see entries VI-73/3 and X-1973-B 3 and 4 in the bibliography which follows.)

Goldmann was the very high level of his moral qualities. This must be emphasized, because the creation and the success of an endeavor always tend toward a particular and rarely attained unity of intellect and character. From this perspective, what compelled admiration for Goldmann was his merging of courage with complete absence of calculation—I would go so far as to say, an absence of all prudence with respect to his own personal interests. This was particularly visible and constant at the outset of his career, at an age when an ordinary man seeking a position takes certain precautions and does not uselessly proclaim anything that could compromise him with persons or milieux which he will have to depend on. But Goldmann always did exactly the opposite. On the one hand, he always insisted on his socialist ideal; on the other, he insisted on his lack of orthodoxy, on his fidelity to the ideals of the young Lukács, and above all, on whatever separated him from the opinions of the majority. Especially at the time his thesis on Jansenism was published, he was in conflict with everyone, as if for the fun of it, although he was not yet a recognized figure it was necessary to deal with. Naturally, the official historians did not take him at all seriously; but, given his heresies, neither did the orthodox Marxists. Yet Goldmann always went forward with undaunted courage, ridiculing compromises and shows of prudence. Finally, it was this force of conviction and independence which made him successful, because in the long run this conduct asserts itself objectively, and because this liberty of spirit and conduct is the prior subjective condition of all true creation.

I trust I may be allowed to mention the beginning of my relations with Goldmann. He arrived one day at my house without announcing himself. He declared that he was a Marxist and that he had therefore come to work with me for a year or two because I was the most authentic dialectician, at least in the West. He had never published anything but had a variety of projects in mind, among them a study of me, etc. In short, at the outset he told me all he could to terrify me—all the more so since I had never witnessed so excessive an enthusiasm. I began to swear at him that I had never read a single word of Marx, nor of Marxist theorists, and that I had no intention of doing so. "All the better," was his response. "I will explain them to you, with none of the deformations or omissions to which Marx's thought is constantly victim." (And in the course of what followed, I was able to determine how much Goldmann's interpretation differed from that of the mainstream commentators.)

He next introduced me to Marxian conceptions on the activity of the subject, which were indeed very remote from the theses of certain

Marxist theorists. He concluded his introductory remarks by seeking to persuade me that I was the only one to have proposed a dialectical vision of the formation of logical structures, of the constitution of number, of those of formal realities which had previously been foreign to dialectical study. If after an hour I engaged Goldmann as a collaborator, it was knowing that, as in the case of his future colleagues, he would teach me more than I could teach him.

In sum, Goldmann is and will remain in history as the inventor or discoverer or a new form of symbolisc thought. Along with the symbolism of a particular individual content (Freudian symbols) or general content (Jungian or, in a sense, Adlerian symbols), and in addition to the myth symbolism which calls for a social but sacred or permanent content, he showed that in theological doctrines such as Jansenism or in literary works such as Racine's plays and the novel, a symbolism existed expressing collective but localized conflicts (between social classes or sub-classes)—and this in their very unfolding and in their specific configuration. Even if certain influences of Lukács are found in his work, it is still true that Goldmann realized a body of facts and theories whose importance will remain essential to the sociology of thought and to epistemology. It is comforting to know that the architect of this work was a man worthy of esteem and sympathy. Such is the tribute that I have wished to render him.

Jean Piaget

APPENDIX 2:

SOME GENERAL COMMENTS ON LUCIEN GOLDMANN

Lucien Goldmann is still much too close to me, too much alive—I cannot attempt to give any kind of "evaluation" of his work, I can only offer some general remarks.

For me, perhaps the most impressive aspect of Goldmann's work was the unity of scholarship and life. To him, philosophy and political radicalism were one, Marxist theory was in the facts themselves; the philosophical and literary documents contained, in themselves, their translation into social reality. "Sociology" was not just one interpretation in addition to others—it was rather the union of all adequate interpretations. Sociology was *in* the philosophical, theological, literary content and form of the works themselves. *Le Dieu cache* is the best example of this union. The book has been criticized on the grounds that it shows an excess of sociological imagination, that Goldmann constructs too freely, etc. I would answer by paraphrasing Adorno's statement on psychoanalysis: that only its exaggerations are true. For it is the extreme point which illuminates the hidden impulses and dimensions of the work.

Similarly in Goldmann's analysis of contemporary literature, especially Malraux, Genet, Robbe-Grillet. Does he interpret too much? I think it is true that the literary substance and the aesthetic form sometimes disappear behind the sociological explication. I was often irritated by it; I used the familiar argument that if the author would have meant all this he would have said so. What was it in the aesthetic form and its exigencies which caused him *not* to say it? We never settled the issue: after lengthy discussions, I felt that Goldmann had made his point—but that I was right too.

Aesthetics is the least developed field in Marxist theory. Goldmann's analysis of the *Nouveau Roman*, the theatre, the film belong to its most advanced contributions. He remains indebted to Lukács, but here too, Goldmann goes his own way. It is the pre-Marxist Lukács, the author of *The Soul and the Forms* and *The Theory of the Novel*, where Goldmann discovers some of the basic concepts of philosophical aesthetics—just as it was Kant rather than Hegel who led him on the road to Marxism.

But prior to all literature and philosophy, Goldmann's Marxism was to him a necessity. He was an eminently political being, and the imperative to change the world was in all his ideas. This imperative was to him a very concrete one, and the social possibilities of its realization had to be examined *in concreto*. He saw in workers' control the most promising vehicle of radical transformation, and he spent much time in studying its practice in Yugoslavia.

I should like to add a few personal remarks.

Goldmann was a radical intellectual who was proud to be an intellectual—without the slightest inferiority complex, so widespread among the New Left, of being a revolutionary and not being a worker. To him, the intellect was by its nature revolutionary. And yet, he was without violence (I never heard him shout) and without malice. Discussion, dialogue were his element. We used to joke: there could not possibly be any conference in his field (and how large was his field!) without Goldmann: Korčula, Cerisy, Brussels, Royaumont, and many others were unthinkable without him. He had to be there, he had to talk: not out of vanity, not because he was egocentric but because discussion and dialogue were to him ways of living with other human beings—ways of finding out, together, what could be done to change things. Strange—but Lucien never showed any signs that he was suffering from the way things were, and yet: I felt he did suffer, but still he smiled, his warm, open smile. I shall never forget an episode (harmless enough) which happened at Korcula. We were all swimming around in the sea; Lucien, who could not swim, was lying on a rubber mat in the water, floating near the beach. Quite suddenly, some of us pulled him off the mat to which he was clinging, and he fell into the water (which was not very deep). He quickly reemerged—heartily laughing with all the others; there was not a trace of resentment in him...

A volume of Goldmann's last papers, published in the

Bibliotheque Mediations,[1] shows on the cover his picture as I remember him so well: his broad open face, his eyes, and his smile. The volume testifies to Goldmann's deep apprehension lest Western society destroy all that was dear to him, to us; that literature and art succumb to the forces of barbarism and a new fascism for a long time to come. Reading these papers, one knows that Goldmann was suffering, but he did not lose his smile of knowledge and hope—his faith in liberation.

Herbert Marcuse

---

1. *La Création culturelle dans la société moderne.*

GOLDMANN AND ADORNO:
TO DESCRIBE, UNDERSTAND AND EXPLAIN

Adorno: Ladies and gentlemen, first of all I would like to say that I am not presenting a prepared exposition, but have come only to learn about the subject of the round table discussions. All that I am going to say will bear the stamp of improvisation.

One preliminary remark. A rigorous dialectical thinker should not in fact speak of method, for the simple reason—which today has almost entirely disappeared from view—that the method should be a function of the object, not the inverse. This notion, which Hegel elaborated very convincingly, is one which has been all too simply repressed by the positivistic spirit, such that the over-valuation of method is truly a symptom of the consciousness of our time. Sociologically speaking, it is closely related to the general tendency to substitute means for ends. In the last instance, this tendency is related to the nature of the commodity: to the fact that everything is seen as functional, as a being-for-another and no longer as something which exists in itself.

It is nevertheless true (and also interesting for the difficulties in which even dialectical thought becomes entangled) that the great texts of modern dialectics, first of all Hegel's *Phenomenology* but also Marx's *Capital*, cannot dispense with methodological reflections. It remains true that method then performed a completely different function: the sole function of allowing the thinker to see clearly what he is and what he is doing. Ideally, at least, this self-reflection should extinguish itself in the object; whereas the ideal of modern scientism is the least problematic, most self-enclosed method, which moves logically as if it were on wheels. It is a method for which the object is secondary in every way.

But it is necessary to insist nonetheless that reflection cannot distort method. In my own work, I have felt constrained again and again by methodological considerations if only to show that certain basic presuppositions of the older methods, such as the succession of a principle by what is derived from it and all the conceptions derived from the ideal notion of a *prima philosophia*, are no longer adequate to dialectical thought. What is needed is a sort of methodology for tracing the limits of traditional thought.

The particular ideas that I wish to set forth about the method of the sociology of literature do not comprise a systematic response to the different problems that my friend Goldmann has raised. I wish to contribute only some marginal notes, and to resist saying things that can be considered more or less self-contained.

First of all, a few words about *description*. I believe that in the literary object certain categories, such as describing and understanding, can never be separated, because each literary text is itself an ensemble of elements that refers to the spirit, whatever its character may be: to be able to describe that, one must understand it. The separation of description and understanding has, then, something completely arbitrary about it that cannot be seriously sustained. But I would like to go still further and add something provocative: I believe that it is not only impossible to describe without understanding, but that, contrary to the dominant opinion, it is impossible to understand without the moment of criticism. If criticism is a moment internal to literature itself, then that is also true for the methodology of reflection about literature: if one takes the concept in its most rigorous sense, *understanding* means nothing but seizing the coherence in the structure of a work and, finally, its *truth content*. But this coherence is possible only as a distinction between coherence and incoherence; and to grasp the truth content always means the ability to distinguish the truth content from the false. Therefore I would say categorically that criticism is always inherent in those categories which, like describing and understanding, appear to be fundamental.

As for the concept of *understanding*, it seems to me that in literary materials, understanding is achieved by levels (I am aware that this recalls an old theological terminology). Thus, if one wishes to understand a play, for example, it is necessary first of all to understand what the situation is. If it is a question of Ibsen's *Wild Duck*, then we first have to understand the elements of the action, the motivation which impels the various characters in their behavior, and all those things which are situated more or less at a factual level but which, in the given play, do not always emerge immediately as factual, are expressed only semantically, and thus have to be deduced.

The second level, then, would be that of what is *signified*. In the case of a psychological drama like *The Wild Duck*, one has to be able to understand, for example, what the poet's intention is in making his characters say certain things. One has to understand that when Hjalmar Ekdal has promised his daughter (who is not his daughter) to bring home the miserable menu of Werle's gala dinner, his forgetting to do so is an act of omission which reveals his character as autistic and basically incapable of love. There are innumerable such elements in this very complex work.

If you will permit me to continue with this play, the third level of understanding would be that of grasping its *idea*. This again comprises several moments. On the one hand, there is the question of concretely developing the concept of the "life-lie" [*Lebenslüge*] which alone allows people to exist. On the other hand, going further, we arrive at the dialectical idea of the play: that the man who tries to eliminate the lie and to base life on veracity and the awareness of reality, succeeds only in causing the greatest unhappiness; and, finally, that the only humane person in the entire play, the only one not entangled in the knot of culpability of the other characters, is victimized precisely by his effort to eliminate the lie.

Traditional literary criticism is habitually content with such moments; but all this is still basically provisional. One of the major errors of current academic literary criticism, aside from its many other errors, seems to be that, in the works it analyzes, it retrieves only what the author has put into them. This is basically a reification of facts which is almost tautological. Great works of art are treated essentially like commercial films—as really nothing more than the quintessence of all the motivations, and, to use a nice expression, of all the "messages," that the malign gentlemen who fabricate such rubbish in their offices have invested in them.

Referring to Thomas Mann, who is a particularly favorite object of this type of literary criticism, I once characterized this business by saying that in his case the essential point is to understand "what is not found in the *Guide Bleu*"—that is, what was not an idea, what was not consciously invested in his work. And it is about this decisive level that I wish to speak now. At issue here is what I would call the *truth content* of a work of art. If I wished to illustrate this point simply by means of *The Wild Duck*, we would have enormous difficulties. But I believe that what in fact decides the aesthetic quality of a work is whether or not it has truth content. I also believe that it is in the truth content, and in it alone, that the contents of works of art communicate with philosophy, but in such a way that it is not found suspended like an abstraction beyond the work. On the contrary, it exists only indirectly; that is, it never exists without the concrete configurations of the pragmatic moments about which I have already spoken.

Let us say for example (just to give you an idea of what I mean, and without claiming to give an adequate determination of the truth content of Ibsen's superb play) that the truth content of this work is the representation of the bourgeois world as one that is always mythical, because of the knot of culpability constituted by the relations of bourgeois society: that it is always basically a question of blind destiny reigning in the somber primitive world, out of which the figure of the child in the play emerges in some ephemeral and feeble way only to become, again in a mythic sense, the victim of this knot of culpability. With this, I have perhaps designated the level that can be called the truth content. But even if it is tied to philosophical concepts such as destiny, myth, culpability, and reconciliation, this does not mean that these concepts are expressed abstractly: they are expressed only by the configuration of elements in this particular play. I speak in this way only to give a general idea of what I mean by truth content.

As for the concept of *explanation*, I would say that it is quite simply the quintessence or the development of those moments about which I have tried to give you a sketchy idea. Such a concept of explanation would include the moment formerly called commentary, as well as the moment of criticism. The explanation of a work would, in effect, take the form of commentary, but it would be impelled to its own consciousness of itself, so that all the levels that I have somewhat arbitrarily set forth and distinguished would enter at this point.

I would still like to speak briefly about the relation between this program and the controversy over "immanent analysis" [*werk-immanente Betrachtung*]. Immanent analysis undoubtedly marks an enormous progress over those philological analyses which were believed to say something essential *about* the works and their truth contents on the basis of their genesis. And I believe you have noted that all the determinations I have given you were oriented first by the concept of an immanent analysis.

But it is necessary to raise some specific points here. First, if one takes seriously the concepts of description and understanding, one cannot start from the presupposition that the understanding reader would be some kind of *tabula rasa*. He himself brings to the works an infinite number of presuppositions, an infinite mass of consciousness. His task consists not simply of forgetting all he brings and making himself a mindless idiot before the work, but instead, of somehow mobilizing all the transcendent knowledge he brings to the work, and making it disappear in the experience of the thing itself during the immanent analysis.

Let me give you a striking example of what I mean, by way of a personal experience. A number of years ago in Los Angeles, I attended a performance of Johann Strauss' *La Chauve souris*, which I had loved so much for its music in Europe. Such a piece is related—not only in terms of its audience, but also in terms of its very form—to many conventions and traditions. When one sees it suddenly detached from its context, in Los Angeles, where no one knows about or even suspects the least "context," which is of course also communicated in the piece itself, then this work, in all its fallibility and feebleness, fades out on an impoverished stage, a bit pitiable and cold. Thinking one is confronted with the piece itself, one does not know what to do with it. This should show us that immanent analysis has an inherent limit which it must necessarily transgress. If I do not bring all these external presuppositions to *La Chauve souris*, I cannot understand it purely in itself; and God knows it is not a difficult masterpiece.

The paradox is that to understand a thing purely in itself, in an immanent way, one must have already seen and known something more than what arises from the thing itself. But this is all the more true for what I have tried to outline, perhaps in a clumsy and insufficient way, as truth content. Truth content is what really transcends the work. In my example I have utilized such concepts as myth, exchange society, knot of culpability, victim—categories which, of course, do not appear in this categorical form in the work. I therefore wish to say that in order to grasp the truth content, that is, to reach the highest level of understanding, one must again transgress the pure immanence of the work of art, just as in the beginning it was necessary to bring pre-immanent knowledge to the immanent work itself in order to master it.

This seems to be to be related to the determination of the work of art, because the work of art has a double character. It is simultaneously a "social fact," and also—and this is precisely what makes it a social fact—something else in relation to reality, something which is against it and somehow autonomous. This ambiguity of art, inasmuch as it belongs to society and inasmuch as it is different from it, leads to the fact that the highest level of art, its truth content and what finally gives it its quality as a work of art, cannot be a purely aesthetic matter. On the contrary, the truth content itself—and this is why I have said that basically only philosophy can grasp it—leads beyond the works precisely because it characterizes the moment of art in which art, in its truth, is more than art. And I believe that to make this dialectic visible, to concretize it in the particular aesthetic experience, would be something like the basis of a program for a method of literary criticism worthy of man; the social moment, the moment of the transcendence of art beyond its own boundaries, should fall like a ripe fruit into the hands of such a criticism.

Goldmann: I believe I am going to put aside my prepared commentary in order to take a position in relation to what Adorno has just said. Yesterday, in front of Agnes Heller, I constantly defended Adorno's positions against the Lukácsian thesis of the realism of the work of art and of the necessity to partake in the sense of history. But today I think I will do the opposite, and establish precisely those points on which I am Lukácsian with respect to Adorno.

The first point is one in which I am in perfect agreement with him: method is not an end in itself. To present method as autonomous is positivism in the worst sense. We discuss method simply insofar as it is subordinated to the thing, to the necessity of comprehending facts; but in the debate with other ideologies, one must pose methodological problems in relation to our own way of understanding the facts. Here perhaps is the first central difference, a disaccord which is not purely accidental, between the positions of the early Lukács and those of Adorno. I agree with Adorno, first, on the fact that true description, the only scientifically valid description, is a comprehensive one. Description is interesting, valuable, and a viable instrument of research, only insofar as it enables us to understand. But when I externally separated description from understanding, it was because today we have the entire structuralist school which promotes a mode of access to the work which is of a descriptive order, but which renounces understanding.

Adorno: That is very Durkheimian.

Goldmann: It is more than Durkheimian: it is a descriptive method which gives us structures in which there are simple reversals, relations, and combinations which have no need of meaning. It is in relation to this that we should take our positions; and when I spoke of explanation—and I believe this is where our immediate disagreement lies—I took "explanation" precisely in relation to what transcends the text. Adorno understood explanation in the sense of *"explication de texte"*: explaining the text, commenting on it, etc. He approached the problem of transcendence later. Everything proceeds from this problem of transcendence and our divergence on it. Because when Adorno tells us "one must transcend the text," he has seen absolute transcendence in the critical spirit alone. One transcends the text on the basis of its cultural elements; one understands it in relation to criticism. The most important element for the value of art is the category of *Wahrheitsgehalt* (truth content): a knowledge which is not aesthetic, which surpasses art as art, and which is situated at the level of the general structure of criticism. There is a word Adorno has not used—"system"—and this is the whole difference between us. Along the same lines, Adorno has said in relation to genetic study, that the return to the immanence of the work was an unquestionable advance. But that seems profoundly questionable to me personally, as well as to Lukács and all traditional Marxists. It is basically the old discussion between Marx's critique and Bauer's *Kritische Kritik*, resumed on the contemporary level. Of course, Adorno poses the questions in a much more refined and subtle way, but, systematically and philosophically, the question is on this level.

This is the basis on which I would like to approach the problem of the status of the work of art. Adorno tells us that one must surpass the work of art to understand it, but surpass it in the sense of philosophy—of philosophical culture and critical knowledge. My position is exactly the opposite: I would say that there is a close relation and a difference between the work of art and philosophy. The work of art is not philosophical: it is a universe of colors, sounds, words, and concrete characters. There is no death, there is Phaedra dying; there is a table of a certain color, but when the critic speaks of this work of art he must have recourse to concepts. Now—and I would like to begin my exposition here—since every critic, whoever he is, speaks in concepts about a work which is not conceptual, and translates it, there is only one valid translation: its translation in a philosophical system. The work of art is a total universe which gives value, takes a position, describes, and affirms the existence of certain things; when translated, its corollary is a philosophical system. It is not a philosophical culture which transcends the work of art; rather, it is a philosophy on the same plane as the work—and to be on the same plane, philosophy must take a systematic form.

I would say that perhaps the greatest difference between Theodor Adorno and me is that I have always insisted on the necessity of accounting for two parallel elements, dogmatism and criticism, and on the danger of neglecting either of them. I have explained that even on the level of scientific thought, it is impossible to bypass the creation of objects. Correlating certain sensations involved in creating an object, and from that, creating world views and systems —this is the order of dogmatism, introduced by the spirit in order to orient itself.

In response, impelled to the extreme limit, the critical spirit denies the very existence of the object—of this chair, for example. Thus, dogmatism involves the clear danger of wishing to conserve at any price systems no longer adapted to reality, but also the danger of not maintaining a critical spirit of confrontation with each system: not discussing the fact that although this system is adapted to the immediate reality, it is still possible to go beyond it because, as "dogma," as a creation of the spirit, and as a world view, it has only a provisional character. But the two elements are always there. And although Lukács (the Lukács of today, not the early Lukács) can be reproached for having accepted one element, one can clearly also raise the problem of the excess of critical spirit, the refusal of system, which may be quite useful at a given moment but cannot be defended on the philosophical level.

Works of art and philosophy are on the same plane; and—perhaps Adorno will agree with me here—I would reproach all the different forms of academic criticism, all forms of positivism, psychologism, and biographical or thematic explication, for underplaying the critical and oppositional aspects of works by rendering them and translating them in terms of concepts on the level of psychology or scientific knowledge. When one says that what matters, what constitutes the conceptual translation, say, of a novel, is the psychology of the characters, the social description, or the set of themes it manifests, one eliminates precisely what this work possesses as a world view—that is, as a questioning and a problematic of human life: in short, one impoverishes the work. The fundamental principle of all academic criticism is precisely to underplay a work's social, humanistic, and spiritual function. This function is critical but also dogmatic, in the sense that dogmatism is the affirmation in each work of a human ideal, of the full possibilities of unity in human life. The relation of this kind of criticism to the work itself is precisely on the order of science, which conveys many cardinally important partial truths; on the other hand, a world view not only constitutes an assertion of a truth but is a precise reflection, a questioning of the entire world.

On this basis, I am much more in agreement with Adorno, though with a slight difference, nevertheless, in relation to all he has said about understanding..

I gladly accept all he has said about different levels if it is added that the first stages are *partial* ones and, as such, are incomplete and false inasmuch as everything partial is false. Adorno said this himself at the end. Simply understanding the characters, the author's intentions, and so forth, is to impoverish and falsely understand the work: it is only in the global understanding of its meaning as a whole work that we can integrate all the other levels. But then— since this is what matters to Adorno—it is not a question of judging the work only on the level of its truth content. Art is art, literature is literature; it is nothing more. It corresponds to philosophy only at the level of its world view. Even if I consider a philosophy entirely erroneous—if I completely reject the philosophy of Bergson or Schelling—this does not prevent it from being one of the basic possibilities, and I do not judge it on the same level as Darwin's theory. I can say that Aristotle's physics is obsolete, but I simply cannot say that his system is obsolete and no longer interests us. Like the artistic work (and like praxis as well), the philosophical work has two languages that are different but are on the same plane, and it affirms fundamental human possibilities in which there are clearly truth contents; but truth content is not the only thing. I would say that it is intellectualism to make these truth contents the essential element. Besides, the important problem is to ask: truth content in relation to what? To the work itself. Because I can certainly believe that Bourdieu or Viggiani or I have the truth, but it requires a control. The problem of the critical spirit is first of all the criticism of my own position; and this control amounts to nothing if it is not scientific and empirical. I am against all positivism which believes that a fact is a fact, and that the human spirit is not involved in its definition; but in order to ascertain the truth content or affirmation of a work, I know of no other criterion than that of taking the text and finding a structure, a model—and here we come to the problem of the generative model—which permits us to account for ninety per cent of the text. If someone succeeds in accounting for ten lines more, we have to ask if his model is not better. It is impossible to say "this is essential; that is unimportant," because only when the interpretation has been established in a purely quantitative manner (knowing that the quantitative does not suffice: this is the dialectical circle) can I say what interpretation is the most valuable, the most objective one possible at the present stage of research. Only then can I say that in this work, independently of the writer's intention, this is essential and that is secondary. And at this point, the problem of explanation arises.

Explanation takes place not on the level of what I myself judge to be an important philosophical element, but in relation to the social structure which I should also comprehend in its systematic structuration. That is, I explain the work—precisely, I transcend it—not by means of philosophical knowledge, by my perspective, or by the elements of the work, but by the structure in which all these are inserted. I explain Racine by Jansenism, through understanding Jansenism as a structure. Explanation is a very precise, comprehensive—and functional—mode of placing things into a relationship. Just as I understand a cat's behavior in catching a mouse, as a function of its hunger, so I understand a literary or artistic work (one I have studied empirically, at the level of the text) as a totality in itself, equivalent to and on the same level as the philosophical work, by placing the work in functional relation with an ensemble of facts, a global structuration, which explains to me how it was born. I understand this work, then, as a function of human aspirations within a given social structure; I understand, too, that this function can itself be recurrent as a human possibility, and that as such (even if I do not agree with it, even if I believe that its *Wahrheitsgehalt* is very feeble today), it can one day return in another situation—all this because in the end, the number of world views is limited and corresponds to basic human positions.

In this sense (here I would agree with Adorno), the only valuable description is a comprehensive one. Without this, one arrives at a general scheme in which, when I grasp the structure of all stories or all novels, I lose what is specific to the tales of Perrault or Anderson, or the novels of Cervantes or Stehdahl—I lose what is nonetheless very important to distinguish. It is necessary, then, that description embrace the ensemble and that it be comprehensive. But, in the second place, my response is precise: in principle and in the abstract, I can conceive of understanding ninety percent of a text by considering it immanently, if one has a certain degree of cultural knowledge; but in reality, I don't know of any instance of this. In fact, such results, which I have obtained in a number of cases, come only through a genetic explanation—that is, through inserting the work in a more global systematization, a vaster significative structure. Here I will simultaneously express my respect, my admiration and my reservation with regard to Adorno's analyses. Adorno has immense cultural knowledge, an immense intuitive capacity; whenever I have read him about a given writer I realize he has brilliant perceptions to which we must recur. When I study an author, I read Adorno's texts as raw material, because he sees partial significations; but, although I do not know all of his work, I believe he never ties himself down to taking a writer work by work, passage by passage—to analyzing an opus in its systematization, in terms of what is inevitably systematic in it. When I taught in Berlin, a whole group of Adorno's students reproached me for being a positivist. I am not a positivist, but I am very positive: the thesis I wish to establish is that to achieve a positive understanding of ninety per cent of a text in research, one must maintain control, step by step. Even if I am convinced that this control will lead to simple confirmations, the critical insertion should be on a level where I can understand and explain at the same time. This is the fundamental problem.

I believe that all of Adorno's remarks—this is his great merit in relation to traditional criticism—tend to investigate the philosophical content, to make a conceptual translation of the work. But he situates this content in relation to his philosophy, in relation to the critical spirit of today, and not in relation to the dogmatic affirmation, tied to its own time, which the work may contain. One can of course judge this affirmation later, but, from the outset, it is the work's proper aesthetic dimension, which is situated on the same level as philosophy or politics (this is the central idea Heidegger took from Lukács, at the price of deforming it). There is no subordination of either the aesthetic or the philosophical with respect to the other; whereas intellectualsm, or the critical position, is always oriented toward a subordination of art to truth.

Now, very briefly, some points which seem important to specify in relation to the discussion of yesterday and this morning. Greimas told me that he does not understand—that he would like to understand but cannot—what the problem of the collective subject could mean at the level of positive science. I respond with the simplest example possible: this table is heavy, and it takes two people to lift it. So the subject who lifts it is not person A or person B, but A *and* B. The fact that the table has been lifted is understandable only in relation to a collective subject. Confronted with a work of art whose global structure and meaning I disengage, my question will always be the same, or of the same type: in relation to what human group is the work understandable? Because if I pose the question of knowledge in relation to the individual, if I ask about the functionality of a play by Racine in relation to the individual Racine, two basic difficulties appear which nullify this type of research. First, Racine's personality is much too complex for one to be able really to study it scientifically and to show the work's functionality. Secondly, if I could obtain a hypothesis of functionality by these means, it would have nothing to do with the literary or cultural character of the work. It would be a functionality like that of a madman's painting in relation to its creator, or the writing of a mediocre man in relation to his own psychology. The collective subject, on the other hand, is an empirical problem: what is the social group whose global action—which I can study as global action, global tendency, and virtual consciousness [*bezogenes Bewusstsein*]—gives me this type of mental structuration as a functional reality, whose study is absolutely indispensable for understanding the internal structure of the work?

Someone told me that I was not clear enough yesterday on the problem of what constitutes the value of a work of art. I believe this is another point where I differ with Adorno. He tells us that in the last instance, the work's value is its critical function and its *Wahrheitsgehalt*, its truth content. For my part, I still hold the Kantian definition retained and historicized by Lukács in the Hegelian and Marxist sense, of a surmounted tension between an extreme richness and an extreme unity, between a very rich universe and a rigorous structuration. This tension cannot be surmounted in a rigorous structuration, but—this is what I would add now—only by a world view, which is precisely one of the basic possibilities of humankind (this explains why at certain times a similar structuration can reappear). I would differ from Kant (and agree with Hegel and Marx) in saying that the unity is not purely formal, valid in relation to permanent and eternal categories of the human spirit, but that it constitutes a world view which, in the case of the privileged groups which are classes, or in the case of any other groups creating culture, is functional for the life of these human groups in given historical situations. Hegel tells us that this unity is historical, that aesthetic structurations are historical. Hegel ended up subordinating this unity to philosophy and truth; Marx and Lukács broke with him there. In the place of this history of the autonomous spirit, Marx, and after him Lukács, posed the existence of the real history of humans as living beings and as groups who wish to maintain themselves, who wish to exist, and who, in a given situation, with given categories, try to elaborate a functional attitude whose translation for privileged groups is, I repeat, philosophy and art. The work of art thus has a function both analogous to and very different from the individual function Freud saw in the imaginary. Freud explained that the function of the imaginary is to compensate for the frustrations of life through imaginary or symbolic satisfaction. The work of art and the imaginary, then, have a precisely analogous function insofar as the work of art permits the creation of an imaginary world with a rigorous form and structure in relation to the group, which is composed of individuals obliged to make all sorts of life compromises and to introduce all kinds of approximations and mixtures into their aspiration toward coherence in vision and in reality. But whereas in psychoanalysis it is a matter of the individual's circumventing social consciousness to gain the satisfaction society has forbidden him—it is a matter of affirming the individual in relation to the group—in the work of art, on the other hand, this imaginary comprehension helps reinforce the group's consciousness because it is situated specifically in relation to those group aspirations, because it resides not in the possession of objects but in coherence, in the category of totality. Thus it has its specific social function which, in the case of great works of art, is at least partially and sometimes even totally progressive. Social progress, however, can mean two things: the new creation of a new order, the aspiration to an order appropriate to the new group or, if the group is conservative, the conservation of the old order; but also the rejection of the groups one opposes, a rejection of oppression and frustrations, and also of structures that correspond to a past and no longer correspond to immediate actuality. In this sense, nothing is more important in scientific thought, in philosophy and in the work of art, than this necessary equilibrium between structuration, the ordering process which according to the critical spirit is, if you wish, dogmatism (perhaps the word dogmatism is not the right choice; I should say rationality), and the opposition that is criticism.

Adorno: If I have understood clearly, the first criticism Goldmann addressed to me was that on the last level I mentioned in my sketch, at the level concerning the truth content of the work, I would illegitimately, surreptitiously, beguilingly introduce the pure subjectivity of criticism.

Goldmann: That was not the most important thing. The first point was that you introduced the truth content as going beyond art.

Adorno: Yes.

Goldmann: You situated transcendence in knowledge, in the surplus of knowledge and not outside this knowledge; thus in the final analysis art becomes knowledge and is not placed on the same level as philosophy; like criticism, philosophy becomes, if you will, an assertion.

Adorno: No, there I have been misunderstood. What I wanted to say was that by the intermediary of truth content, art and philosophy converge.

Goldmann: I have not misunderstood. All I said was this: you said that one cannot understand without being critical, and that transcendence is situated in the critical consciousness, in the element and not in the system.

Adorno: I would like to respond specifically to this point. That transcendence beyond the work of art lies in the work itself. I could cite Goethe's phrase in the journal of Ottilie in *Elective Affinities*, that everything perfect transcends its genre: that is exactly what I mean to say. By its participation in the truth content, the work of art is more than what it is, and what the knowledge of art should do is explain—in some way imparting this movement in the work of art—what is crystalized in the work itself. I would not wish to say that this is a question of conceptual truth, for, on the one hand, truth as we find it in philosophy and the sciences, insofar as it is concept, entirely overlooks the fact that, on the one hand, it is present in the work of art—but only, if you will, blindly present. And the idea of the truth itself is something that probably can be grasped only in a fragmentary manner.

Goldmann: What does it mean to say that it is there blindly, that it is not conceptual, that it is not conscious? My question, ther—to end the discussion of what has been said and get to the discussion at hand—is this: can the work of art be great even if its validity on the plane of conceptual translation, of conceptual truth, is very feeble?

Adorno: No. On this point, I would say categorically no. A work of art which, in this extreme sense, has no truth content, cannot be conceived as a true work of art.

Goldmann: The definition of truth remains to be known, of course. Who judges the truth?

Adorno: The point is that the movement of truth is objective. But first, the question of system. I would say that the work of art is in a certain sense a system, in that it is a self-enclosed unity of a multiplicity. But at the same time, works of art are always the contrary of a system as well: insofar as we live in an antagonistic society, by virtue of its pragmatic presuppositions, no work of art can entirely achieve this unity. And it is precisely at this point that I would interpose the question of the rank or quality of works of art. I would say that the rank or the quality of works of art is measured—if one can employ this flat term—according to the degree in which antagonisms are formed within the work of art, and in which their unity is attained through antagonisms rather than remaining external to them.

Goldmann: Allow me to make a proposal. We have some language difficulties, but since I believe we still have time, I will discuss this point in German with Adorno before we begin again tomorrow.

Adorno: There are some points to which I would like to resond quickly, despite the semantic difficulties.

Goldmann: Then, another question. Hegel: is this a system? It is a system which integrates antagonisms on the plane of philosophy.

Adorno: It integrates them too much.

Goldmann: Perhaps, but nevertheless, it is a great system, which does not eliminate antagonisms. If it is necessary to take a concrete writer, then let's look at Beckett, on whom Adorno has worked so much. It think that if someday I were to do a study on Beckett (I have already worked on writers of the same epoch, Genet and Gombrowicz; the same could be done with Beckett), I would probably end up showing that where it is great, Beckett's work integrates antagonisms, difficulties, and fragments within a world view which is global and that can, despite everything else, be reduced to a system. I believe there is no opposition between the two views, and that in the face of the danger Adorno indicates—which is real enough—of the superficial system which simplifies and eliminates antagonisms, there is the other danger of criticism which consists in eliminating the system.

Adorno: I wish to add only one thing. Those works of art most fully achieving unity in multiplicity do not by any means automatically have the highest value. There are some works of art which precisely by their fragmentary character—and I consider the fragment as a form—raise themselves above this systematic unity and have qualities which surpass unity. I will mention only Beethoven's last quartets; I could also cite certain of Goethe's last works in which—and for very profound reasons—this unity is suspended. More precisely, I believe that, in fact, this suspension of unity in multiplicity in works of a very high level is somehow the point or lacuna through which their truth content appears in them.

I would also like to say a word about the concepts of meaning and incomprehensibility. You have said that in art there are structures which one must accept as such, and which are not properly speaking understandable.

Goldmann: I said that this is why I disagree with the structuralists.

Adorno: Then it is structuralism that makes this claim.

Goldmann: Structuralism seeks structures without demanding that they have meaning. One describes structures, but functional meaning disappears.

Adorno: I would say that it is precisely at this point that the problem of significant advanced modern art is situated. For radical modern art—and not only literature—is that which, in opposition to the affirmative moment of traditional art, refuses meaning: that which has deprived itself of meaning and which *presents itself as destitute of meaning*. But in such works, one can understand the function of the negation of meaning: here, the negation of meaning is the very meaning. And this is why, in full awareness of the issue, I have entitled a work on Beckett, "Essay on Understanding *End-game*." To understand means not that one understands the function of the incomprehensible. At this point, in fact, I see a limit to the liqui-incomprehensible. At this point, in fact, I see a limit to the liqui-dation of meaning, and I believe that if it is true that structuralism simply renounces all meaning, then it falls back to a level this side of art, to a pre-aesthetic level.

Still another word on the relation between philosophy and art. What I have called the truth content is found in the work of art only insofar as it is mediated—only insofar as it arises through the structure of the work itself, and not conceptually. But what emerges in this manner in fact converges with philosophy and, by this means, with all extra-aesthetic reality, including society and political praxis.

A last word on the problem Lucien has raised about the relation between my particular analyses and fundamental theoretical works. All I can say is that I have tried to articulate this relation in my theoretical writings. But whether and how well I have succeeded in that is certainly not for me to decide; there my little analyses must stand on their own feet and defend themselves.

Goldmann: To speak very briefly, Adorno has raised three points. On the first, on structuralism and meaning, I am in complete agreement. As for the fragment, I admit that a work is often very valuable when it is fragmentary—I have twice analyzed fragments (Pascal's *Pensées*, and Valéry's *Fragments*)—but in each case, it is a question of placing this fragmentary character in the totality of the work which is translated into a system. There is no opposition between system and fragment; in the philosophical translation, a fragment can be an element of systemization.

On the last point, there is a misunderstanding which we must discuss together. I did not say what Adorno thought I said; the objection was not at all on that count.

LUCIEN GOLDMANN:

A BIBLIOGRAPHY

This compilation draws on four earlier bibliographies: two brief lists by Franco Crispini and Laurent Le Sage, and two extensive ones by Brigitte Navelet and Eduard Tell (see bibliographical entries VIII-1a and XV-4; see especially VIII-1a and 3d and X-1973-B-15).

Tell's bibliography is indebted to Navelet's, but it contains a wealth of detail for each entry. Our own effort is modelled on Tell's, but it reduces the information per item, adds a few entries from Navelet that Tell missed, and adds selections and data from Crispini and Le Sage, as well as from our own resources. Most importantly, we have added the list of English language translations of Goldmann and a short checklist of criticism of Goldmann in English. We make no claims for exhaustiveness on the basis of our additions, although this bibliography probably contains the largest number of listings on Goldmann to date. It is only to be hoped that our effort contributes to a more complete bibliography of Goldmann in English that may emerge in the future.

We have modelled our format on Tell's. Sections I through VII set forth a complete list of Goldmann's publications. Sections VIII through XII offer a broad sampling of criticisms and applications of Goldmann in Europe (mainly in French, Spanish and Italian). Sections XIII and XIV provide a list of Goldmann's books and articles in English, while Sections XV and XVI present examples from the ever-growing number of English language works dealing with or involving Goldmann. Since a few of Goldmann's articles appeared originally in English, we felt it necessary to list them both in the complete list of his publications and in the section on his translated articles (see XIV, 17-20). In every other respect, we have sought to avoid repetition and to keep the bibliography as short as possible.

Thus, in I through VIII, those works which have been translated into English are preceded by an asterisk (*), and the corresponding entry for the translation is coded in the column to the right of the entry. Inversely, in XIII-XIV, numbers in the right column refer to the original listing in I-XII. For example, in Section I we find:

1955 *A. *Le Dieu caché*   XIII-3

Thus, in Section XIII, we find:

3. *The Hidden God*   I-1955-A

Also, in an effort to make the bibliography both useful and short, other entries contain cross reference indications (e.g., "See II-1957-A-3-b"); further, only those periodicals not published in Paris or in the U.S. are listed according to the city of publication. Finally, abbreviations indicated in the following list have been used after first reference has been made to a frequently cited book, periodical, or publisher. The abbreviations are listed in alphabetical order; those referring to books have right column entries indicating their primary location in the bibliography.

Ileana Rodriguez
Marc Zimmerman

ABBREVIATIONS

AESC	*Annales—Economies, sociétés, civilisations*	
BSE	*Bulletin de la société d'étude du XVIIe siècle*	
BSFP	*Bulletin de la société francaise de la philosophie*	
CC	*La Création culturelle dans la société moderne*	I-1971/2-A
CRB	*Les Cahiers de la compagnie Madeleine Renaud—Jean Louis Barrault*	
DC	*Le dieu caché*	I-1955-A
EISULB	Editions de l'Institut de Sociologie de l'Université Libre de Bruxelles	
ENGS	*Entretiens sur les notions de genèse et de structure* (M. Gandillac)	I-1970/1-A-16
EP	*Les Etudes philosophiques*	
ESL	*Etudes de sociologie de la littérature* (EISULB)—a series	
HS	*L'Homme et la société*	
IK	*Introduction à la philosophie de Kant*	I-1947-A-B-C
LG	Sami Nair and Michael Lowy, *Lucien Goldmann ou la dialectique de la totalité*	VIII-3
LH	*Lukàcs et Heidegger*	I-1973-A
MS	*Marxisme et Sciences humaines*	I-1970/2-A
PUF	Presses Universitaires de France	
RA	*Racine*	I-1956-B
RD	*Recherches dialectiques*	I-1959-A
RIS	*Revue de l'institut de sociologie de l'Université Libre de Bruxelles*	
RP	*Raison Présente*	
SCR	*Situation de la critique raciniene*	I-1971/1-A
SHP	*Sciences humaines et Philosophie*	I-1952-A
SM	*Structures mentales et création culturelle*	I-1970/1-A
SR	*Pour une sociologie du roman*	I-1964-A
TDR	*The Drama Review*	
TM	*Les Temps Modernes*	
TP	*Théâtre Populaire*	

I. BOOKS BY GOLDMANN

1947   A. *Mensch, Gemeinschaft und Welt in der Philosophie Immanuel Kants. Studien zur Geschichte der Dialektik.* [*Man, Community and the World in the Philosophy of Immanuel Kant: Studies in the History of Dialectics*]. Zurich, New York: Europea Verlag, 1945. Doctoral thesis presented to the University of Zurich.

B. *La Communauté humaine et l'Univers chez Kant. Etudes sur la pensée dialectique et son histoire.*
Paris: Presses Universitaires de France, 1948. Goldmann's French translation of his German language thesis. Contains a new four-page preface for the French edition, and the following modifications: (a) A short addition to Chapter 1, concerning the social bases for the tragic world view in 17th century France (pp. 23-25 in the 1948 edition, pp. 55-57 in the 1967 edition): (b) The deletion of an appendix about Heidegger and Lukács now seen as peripheral to a study of Kant (see I-1973-A).

1. Chapter 1 of this edition was published separately as "La Philosophie classique et la bourgeoisie occidentale," in *La Revue Socialiste: Culture—doctrine—action*, 12 (new series: June, 1947), pp. 49-64.

*C. *Introduction à la philosophie de Kant*   XIII-1
(new edition of I-1947-B).
Paris: Gallimard, 1967. Adds an important six-page preface, dated May, 1967.

1952   A. *Sciences humaines et Philosophie.* Paris: PUF, 1952.

*B. *Sciences humaines et Philosophie* (*Qu'est-ce que la*   XIII-2
Sociologie?).
Paris: Ed. Gonthier, 1966. Adds an important preface dedicated to the memory of Lucien Sebag.

C. *Sciences humaines et Philosophie* (*Pour un structuralisme génétique*).
Paris: Ed. Gonthier, 1971. Adds a brief but valuable biographical note by Annie Oliver Goldmann (p. 167) and an article:

*1. "Structuralisme génétique et création littéraire"   XIV-1
(pp. 151-65).

1955   *A. *Le Dieu caché. Etude sur la vision tragique dans les*   XIII-3
"Pensées" de Pascal et dans le théâtre de Racine.   (XIV-2)

Paris: N.R.F., Gallimard, 1955. Dissertation presented to the Université de Paris.

1956   A. *Jean Racine, dramaturge.* Paris: L'Arche, 1956.

   *B. *Racine.* Paris: L'Arche, 1970.   XIII-4
      This edition deletes the Bibliographie and the "Répertoire de
      mises en scènes" of the 1956 edition (pp. 149-58).

1959   A. *Recherches dialectiques.* Paris: Gallimard, 1959.
      A collection of articles written or published between 1942 and
      1959, and ordered into three sections, as follows:

      I. *Problèmes de Méthode*
         1. "Le matérialisme dialectique est-il une philosophie?"
            (1947), in *Revue Internationale de Philosophie,* 45-46
            (Brussels, XIIe année, 1958), pp. 249-64.
         2. "Matérialisme dialectique et histoire de la philosophie"
            (1947), in *Revue Philosophique de la France et de l'étranger,*
            4-6 (Paris, April-June, 1948).
        *3. "Matérialisme dialectique et histoire de la   XIV-3
            littérature" (1947), in *Revue de Métaphysique et de Morale,*
            3 (July-Sept., 1950).
         4. "La Réification," in *Les Temps Modernes,* 156-157 (Feb.-
            March, 1959).
         5. "Le concept de structure significative en histoire de la
            culture" (1958), in *Sens et usages du terme Structure dans
            les sciences humaines et sociales* (Paris, The Hague: Mouton
            & Co., 1962).
         6. "La psychologie de Jean Piaget," in *Critique,* 13-14 (June-
            July, 1947).
         7. "L'Epistémologie de Jean Piaget," in *Synthèses,* 82
            (Brussels: 7e annee, March, 1953).
         8. "La nature de l'oeuvre," in *Les Etudes philosophiques,* 3
            (July-Sept., 1957), pp. 139-43. Presentation to the IXe
            Colloque des Sociétés de Philosophie de langue française,
            held at Aix-en-Provence (Sept. 2-5, 1957), on the theme of
            "l'Homme et ses oeuvres."

      II. *Analyses concrètes*
         1. "Vision tragique du monde et noblesse de robe," published
            as "Remarques sur le Jansénisme: la vision tragique du
            monde et la noblesse de robe," in *Bulletin de la "Société
            d'étude du XVIIe siècle,"* 19 (1953), pp. 23-54. (See V-67/1.)
         2. "Le 'Pari' est-il écrit 'pour le libertin'?" (1954), in *Blaise
            Pascal. L'homme et l'oeuvre* (Paris: Ed. de Minuit, 1956).
            (See V-67/1.)

3. *"Bérénice,"* published as *"Bérénice* ou le tragique racinien," in *Théâtre populaire*, 20 (Sept., 1956), text read at the R.T.F. by Sylvia Montfort.
4. *"Phèdre,"* a paper read at l'Ecole de théâtre Jean Deschamps in 1953. (See V-67/1.)
5. *"Phèdre*. Remarques sur la mise en scène," in *Bref*, 11 (Dec., 1957).
6. "Goethe et la Révolution française," in *Etudes germaniques*, 2-3 (1949).
7. "Un grand polémiste: Karl Krauss," in *Lettres*, 4 (Geneva: 3e année, 1945), pp. 166-73.
8. "A propos du 'Karl Kraus' de W. Kraft," in *Allemagne d'aujourd'hui*, 2 (1957).
9. "A propos de *La Maison de Bernarda* de F. Garcia Lorca," in TP, 24 (May, 1957).

III. *Chroniques*
1. "Georges Lukàcs, l'essayiste," in *Revue d'esthétique*, 1 (Jan-March, 1950).
2. "Propos dialectiques," in TM, 137-38 (July-August, 1957).
*3. "Y a-t-il une sociologie marxiste?" published as XIV-4 "Propos dialectiques. Y a-t-il une sociologie marxiste?" in TM, 140 (Oct., 1957), pp. 729-75.
4. "Morale et droit naturel," published as "Propos dialectiques. Morale et droit naturel," in TM, 143-44 (Jan.-Feb., 1958).
5. "Problèmes de théorie critique de l'économie," published as "Propos dialectiques. Problèmes de théorie critique de l'économie," in TM, 148 (May-June, 1958).
6. "Postface" (1959), pp. 343-53.

1964 A. *Pour une Sociologie du Roman*. Paris: Gallimard, 1964. (See II-63.) Contains:
1. "Préface" (June, 1964).
*2. "Introduction aux problèmes d'une sociologie du XIV-5 Roman," which appeared first in *Revue de l'Institut de Sociologie*, 2 (Brussels, 1963), pp. 225-42. (See II-63-A.)
3. "Introduction à une étude structurale des romans de Malraux," which also appeared in RIS, 2, pp. 285-393; part of this text was also published as "L'individu, l'action et la mort dans *Les Conquerants* de Malraux," in *Médiations*, 6 (Summer, 1963), pp. 69-94. (See II-63-A.)
4. "Nouveau roman et realité." This study brings together two earlier works: a paper read at a discussion with Nathalie Sarraute and Robbe-Grillet (see II-63-A) and an analysis of Robbe-Grillet's novels, published in *Mediations*, 4 (1962).

*5. "La méthode structuraliste génétique en histoire de   XIV-6
la littérature," published as "Le structuralisme génétique en
histoire de la littérature," *Modern Language Notes*, 79/3
(May, 1964), pp. 225-34.

*B. *Pour une Sociologie du Roman*. Paris: Gallimard, 1965.   XIII-5
Most additions to the 1964 version are set forth in a preface note
(p. 16), dated April, 1965: (a) Three footnotes (pp. 277, 313, and
362): (b) A study of a recent film by Robbe-Grillet, written with
Anne Olivier and first published as "L'Immortelle est de retour,"
in *L'Observateur* (Sept. 18, 1964): (c) This edition also contains
some important comments added to the last chapter (pp. 365-72),
which do not appear in the 1964 version (or in the original English
language version [XIV-6]).

1970/1 A. *Structures mentales et création culturelle*. Paris: Anthropos,
1970. (See II/69.) Contains:

1. Preface (Paris: July, 1970).
*2. "La philosophie des Lumières," trans. by Irene Petit   XIII-6
from the German original of 1960, *Der Christliche Bürger
und die Aufklärung* [*The Christian Bourgeoisie and the Enlightenment Thinkers*] (Neuwied and Berlin: Hermann
Luchterhand Verlag, 1968). A French translation of part of
this text appeared as "La pensée des 'Lumières'," in
Annales—Economies, Sociétés, Civilisations, 4 (XXIIe
année, July-Aug., 1967).
3. "Le probleme du mal: A propos de *'Rodogune'* et de
'l'Annonce faite à Marie'," in *Médiations*, 3 (1961).
4. "Valéry et la dialectique: A propos de *'Mon Faust'*," in
Médecine de France, 163 (1965).
5. "Valéry: *Monsieur Teste*," paper presented at l'ORTF,
1965; appeared (in French) in *Critical Spirit: Essays in
Honor of Herbert Marcuse*, ed. Kurt H. Wolff and
Barrington Moore, Jr. (Boston: Beacon Press, 1967).
6. "Les deux avant-gardes," in *Médiations*, 4 (1961).
*7. "Problèmes philosophiques et politiques dans le   XIV-7
théâtre de Jean-Paul Sartre. L'itineraire d'un penseur," in
L'Homme et la société, 17 (1970).
*8. "Le théâtre de Gombrowicz," *Paragone*, Nuova   XIV-8
Serie, 32 (Florence, 1967).
9. "A propos d'*Operette* de Gombrowicz," in *La Quinzaine
Littéraire*, 88 (Jan. or Feb. 1-15, 1970).
10. "Le théâtre de Genet. Essai d'étude sociologique," in
Contributions à la Sociologie de la connaissance (Paris:
Anthropos, 1967), preface by Roger Bastide, pp. 109-40.

This text, Goldmann's most complete article on Genet's theatre, contains a passage on *The Blacks* (pp. 130-32) not published in the version appearing in RIS, 3 (see II/69); it is a development of materials set forth in a paper read at Cologne (Westdeutschen Rundfunk, 1966), published as:

*a. "L. Goldmann: Le théâtre de Genet et ses études   XIV-9 sociologiques," CRB, 57 (Nov., 1966), pp. 90-123.

11. "Microstructures dans les vingt-cinq premières répliques des *Nègres* de Jean Genet," written in collaboration with Agnes Caers, Willy Delsipech, Jean-Michel Hennebert, Roger-Jean Lallemand and Pierre Vertraeten. First appeared in *Modern Language Notes*, 5 (Vol. 82, 1967), and then in RIS, 3 (1969), pp. 363-80.

12. "*Eloges III* de Saint-John Perse," written with the same group as "Microstructures" (see I-70/1-11), in RIS, 3 (1969).

13. "La Gloire des Rois, de Saint-John Perse," in *ibid.*

14. " 'Les Chats' de Baudelaire," written with Norbert Peters, in *ibid.*

15. "Notes sur deux romans de Marie-Claire Blais," in *ibid.*

16. "Sur la peinture de Chagall. Réflexions d'un sociologue." Paper based on one presented at a conference organized by the VIe section of the Ecole Pratique des Hautes Etudes (Cérisy-la-Salle: July-Aug., 1959), and published as "A propos de quelques réflexions structuralistes sur la peinture de Chagall," in Gandillac, Goldmann, *et al., Entretiens sur les notions de genèse et de structure* (Paris, The Hague: Mouton & Co., 1965); published under the present title in *Annales*, 4 (July-Aug., 1960), pp. 667-93.

17. "Réponse a MM. Elsberg et Jones," in RIS, 3 (1969).

18. "Réponse a MM. Daix et Picard," *ibid.*

19. "Le Dieu caché, la nouvelle critique et le marxisme," in TM, 134 (March, 1957).

1970/2 A. *Marxisme et Sciences humaines.* Paris: Gallimard, 1970.

Contains:

1. "Préface" (Sept., 1970): reprinted as "Le testament théorique de Goldmann," in LG (VIII-3), pp. 127-34.

2. "Genèse et Structure" (1959), in ENGS.

*3. "Critique et dogmatisme dans la création littéraire"   XIV-10 (1967). Appeared in English first.

*4. "La sociologie de la littérature: statut et   XIV-11 problèmes de méthode," first published as "Sociologie de la littérature: situation actuelle et problèmes de méthode," in *Revue Internationale des sciences sociales, UNESCO*, 4 (Vol. XIX, 1967).

5. "Le sujet de la création culturelle." Paper given at the second colloquium of Sociologie de la Littérature, organized by the Institut de Sociologie de L'ULB and the Ecole Pratique des Hautes Etudes (VIe section) de Paris with the assistance of UNESCO, on the theme "Critique sociologique et critique psychanalytique" (Royaumont, Dec. 10-12, 1966). Published in various places:
   a. *Revue de sociologie* (Montreal: Université de Montréal, 1967).
   b. HS, 6 (1967).
   c. *Critique Sociologique et Critique Psychanalytique* (Brussels: EISULB, 1970), pp. 193-211.
6. "Conscience réele et conscience possible. Conscience adequate et fausse conscience." Paper presented at the IVe Congrès Mondial de Sociologie, 1959.
7. "Philosophie et sociologie dans l'oeuvre du jenue Marx," in *Annali dell'Instituto Giangiacomo Feltrinelli* (Milan, 7th year, 1964-65).
*8. "L'Idéologie allemande et les Thèses sur Feuerbach," in HS, 7 (1968).   XIV-12
9. "Economie et sociologie: A propos du 'Traité d'Economie politique' d'Oscar Lange," in HS, 14 (1969).
10. "Pour une approche marxiste des études sur le marxisme," in AESC, 1 (1963).
*11. "L'esthetique du jeune Lukàcs," in *Médiations*, 1 (1961).   XIV-13
12. "Jean-Paul Sartre: Question de méthode," in *L'Annee sociologique* (Paris: PUF, 1961).
*13. "Reflexions sur la pensée de Herbert Marcuse," in *La Nef.* 36 (Jan.-Mar., 1969).   XIV-21
*14. "Socialisme et humanisme," in Diogène, 46 (Apr.-June, 1964).   XIV-14
15. "De la rigeur et de l'imagination dans la pensée socialiste" (1964), in *Praxis*, 2-3 (Zagreb, 1965).
16. "Pouvoir et humanisme" (1969), in *Praxis*, 1-2 (1970).

1971/1   A. *Situation de la critique racinienne.* Paris: L'Arche, 1971. Contains a bibliographical note by Annie Goldmann, which also appears in Zima (see VIII-4-a), pp. 125-127.

1971/2 *A. La Création culturelle dans la societe moderne*   XIII-7 (*Pour une sociologie de la totalité*). Ed. Denoël Gonthier, 1971. This pothumously published volume contains:

1. "L'importance du concept de conscience possible pour la communication," in *Le concept d'information dans la science contemporaine,* Cahiers de Royaumont. Gauthier

Villars/Editions de Minuit, 1965.
2. "Possibilités d'action culturelle à travers les mass-media"
(1967). Paper presented at the international seminar on
mass media and imaginative creation organized by Jean
Duvignaud under the sponsorship of the Institut de
Sociologie de l'Art (Faculté des Lettres de Tours) and the
Association Internationale pour la Liberté de la Culture, the
CINI Foundation (Venice: Oct., 1967).
3. "La révolte des lettres et des arts dans les civilisations
avancées" (1968), in *Liberté et organisation dans le monde
actuel*, Desclée de Brouwer (Brussels), pp. 245-79.
4. "Les interdependances entre la société industrielle et les
nouvelles formes de la création littéraire" (1965). Not
previously published.
5. "Pensée dialectique et sujet transindividual," in *Bulletin de
la Société Française de Philosophie*, 3 (64e année, July-
Sept., 1970).
6. "La dialectique aujourd'hui" (1970), in HS, 19 (Jan.-March,
1971). Paper given at the Summer School of Korčula, Yugoslavia, August, 1970.

1973   A. *Lukàcs et Heidegger. Fragments posthumes établis et presentés
par Youssef Ishaghpour.* Paris: Ed. Denoël, 1973. Contains:
(a) An "Avant-propos" by Ishaghpour (pp. 5-56): (b) an "Introduction à Lukàcs et Heidegger," begun in Aug., 1970, which,
though unfinished, has been published as is: (c) Goldmann's
lecture comments during the 1967-8 university year, recorded and
ordered by the editor. (See I-1947-B and V-73/4).

II. COLLECTIVE WORKS PUBLISHED UNDER
GOLDMANN'S DIRECTION

Collections from the series, *Etudes de sociologie de la littérature*
(ESL I-IV).

1963   A. *Problèmes d'une sociologie du roman.* RIS, 2 (ESL I, 1963).
Contains what will constitute Chapters 1-3 of PSR (I-1964A 2-4),
pp. 225-42, 285-92, 449-67, including commentaries by Robbe-
Grillet and Sarraute on Goldmann's critique. Also contains
articles by G. Lukàcs, R. Girard, E. Kohler and M. Bernard.
There are two editions of this volume.

1967   A. *Littérature et Société. Problèmes de méthodologie en sociologie
de la littérature.* EISULB (ESL II, Brussels, 1967). Contains
articles and discussions from the first international colloquium on

sociology and literature, held in Brussels (May 21-23, 1964) and organized by the Institut de Sociologie de l'ULB and the sixth section of Ecole Pratique des Hautes Etudes of Paris. Goldmann's contribution is the article:

> *1. "Le structuralisme génétique en sociologie   XIV-15 de la littérature," pp. 195-211. The article is followed by excerpts from the discussion it provoked, pp. 211-22.

Also contains presentations by A. Doucy, L. Sanguinetti, R. Barthes, E. Kohler, G. Mouillaud, A. Silbermann, H. Lefebvre, F. Brun, Ch. Aubrun, R. Escarpit, B. Dort and J. Kott.

1969   A. *Sociologie de la Littérature. Recherches récentes et discussions.* RIS, 3 (ESL III, 1969). Contains articles which appear later in SM (I-1970/1 A-10-15, 17-18). Also contains an article not included in SM:

> 1. "Note sur quatre films de Godard, Buñuel et Pasolini," pp. 475-77.

For articles in this volume by Goldmann's students and colleagues, see X-1969-A. A reprint of this volume under the same title appeared in 1970.

1970   A. *Critique sociologique et critique psychanalytique.* EISULB (ESL IV, Brussels, 1970). Contains:

> 1. "Le sujet de la création culturelle," pp. 193-211; appears later in MS (I-1970/2-A-5).

Also contains presentations by R.Bastide, S. Doubrovsky, U. Eco, R. Girard, Ch. Mauron, P. Ricoeur, etc.

III. WORKS EDITED BY GOLDMANN

1956   A. *Correspondance de Martin de Barcos, Abbé de Saint-Cryan, avec les abbesses de Port-Royal et les principaux personnages du groupe janséniste.* Paris: PUF, 1956.
Complementary thesis for the Doctor of Letters, edited and presented by Goldmann to the Faculté des Lettres de l'Université de Paris; published under the auspices of the Centre National de la Recherche Scientifique.

IV. TRANSLATIONS BY GOLDMANN

1948   Jean Piaget, *Psychologie der Intelligenz*, German translation of *Psychologie de l'intelligence* by Lucien Goldmann and Yvonne Mauser (Zürich: Rascher Verlag, 1948).

1949/1   G. Lukàcs, *Goethe et son époque*, French trans. by André Frank and Lucien Goldmann (Paris: Nagel, 1949).

1949/2   G. Lukàcs, *Brève histoire de la littérature allemande du XVIIIe siècle a nos jours*, French trans. by Michel Butor and Lucien Goldmann (Paris: Nagel, 1949).

1970   G. Lukàcs, *Novalis et la philosophie romantique de la vie*, French trans. by Lucien Goldmann, in *Romantisme. Revue de la société des études romantiques*, 1-2 (1971). Translation of one of the articles contained in *Die Seele und die Formen* (Berlin: Fleishel, 1911), pp. 81-91.

V. ARTICLES IN PERIODICALS AND COLLECTIVE VOLUMES

48/1   "Les conditions sociales et la vision tragique du monde," in *Echanges Sociologiques*, ed. Cercle de Sociologie de la Sorbonne, Centre de Documentation Universitaire (Paris, 1948), pp. 81-91.

50/1   "Pascal et la pensée dialectique," in *Empedocle. Revue littéraire mensuelle*, 7 (2e annee, Jan., 1950), pp. 47-61.

52/1   "Thèses sur l'emploi du concept de vision du monde en histoire de la philosophie," in *L'Homme et l'Histoire*: Actes du VIe congres des Sociétés de philosophie de langue française (Strasbourg, Sept. 10-14, 1952) (Paris: PUF, 1952).

53/1   "Remarques sur la théorie de la connaissance," in *Epistémologie/Epistemology*: Actes du XIe Congrès International de Philosophie (Brussels, Aug. 20-234, 1953) (Amsterdam: North Holland Publishing Company; Louvain: E. Nauwelaerts, 1953), pp. 90-95.

54/1   "Au sujet du 'plan' des *Pensées* de Pascal," in BSE, 23 (3e trimestre, 1954), pp. 597-602.

55/1   "*Port-Royal* d'Henri Montherlant, mise en scène de Jean Meyer a la Comédie-Française," in TP, 11 (Jan.-Feb., 1955), pp. 86-88.

57/1 "*L'hôtel du libre échange* de Georges Feydeau et Marie Desvallières, avec la compagnie Grenier-Hussenot, au Théâtre Marigny," in TP, 22 (Jan., 1957), p. 87.

57/2 "Un bilan désabusé. A propos de Fritz Sternberg: *Kapitalismus und Sozialismus vor dem Weltgericht: Marx und die Gegenwart,*" in *Arguments*, 1 (1re année, Feb.-March, 1957).

57/3 "Philosophie et scientisme," in *Chacun peut-il philosopher?* 9e conférence-debat de Cercle ouvert (Paris: La Nef, 1957). Also contains contributions by L. Althusser, F. Chatelet, G. de Gandillac, J. Wahl, etc.

57/4 "La nature de l'oeuvre," in EP, 3 (1957). Actes du IXe congrès des sociétés de philosophie de langue francaise (l'Homme et ses oeuvres).

57/5 "Quelques remarques sur la philosophie de T.W. Adorno," in *Allemagne d'aujourd'hui*, 6 (Nov.-Dec., 1957), pp. 94-96. Review of Adorno's *Aspekte der Hegelschen Philosophie* (1957).

57/6 "Réponse de Lucien Goldmann," in TM, 142 (Dec., 1957), pp. 1141-44. Goldmann answers M. Rubel's "Mise au point non dialectique," *ibid.*, pp. 1138-41, which in turn is an answer to Goldmann's review of Rubel's *Karl Marx—Essai de biographie intellectuelle* (Paris: Marcel Riviere, 1957), "Y a-t-il une sociologie marxiste?" (See I-1959-A-III-3.)

58/1 "*Faust*, de...," in TP, 32 (43 trimestre, 1958), pp. 139-40.

59/1 "L'apport de la pensée marxiste a la critique littéraire," in *Arguments*, 12-13 (3e année, Jan.-March, 1959), pp. 44-46.

60/1 "Liberté et valeur" (1958), in *Atti del XII Congresso Internazionale di Filosofia*, Şept. 12-18, 1958, vol. III: *Libertà e valore?* (Florence: Editore Sansoni, 1950), pp. 183-85.

60/2 "Préface nouvelle" to Jean Juares, *Les origines du socialisme allemande*, trans. from Latin by Adrien Veber (Paris: Maspero, 1960).

60/3 "*Phèdre*, de Racine et *Nathan le Sage*, de Lessing, mises en scene de H.K. Zeiser et K.H. Stroux, avec le Schauspielhaus de Düsseldorf, au Théâtre des Nations," in TP, 38 (2e trimestre, 1960), pp. 110-11.

60/4 "Etre et dialectique," in EP, 2 (Apr.-June, 1960), pp. 205-212.

60/5   "Une pièce réaliste: *Le Balcon* de Genet," in TM, 171 (June, 1960), pp. 1885-96.

60/6   "Jean Juares, la question religieuse et le socialisme," in *Bulletin de la société d'études juaresiennes*, 1 (1re année, June, 1960), pp. 6-12.

61/1   "Civilisation et économie" (July 14, 1958), in *L'Histoire et ses interprétations. Entretiens autour de Arnold Toynbee sous la direction de Raymond Aron* (Paris, The Hague: Mouton & Co., 1961), pp. 76-90; followed by a discussion with R. Aron, L. Sebag, A. Toynbee, etc. Ecole Pratique des Hautes Etudes de Paris (sixth section).

61/2   "Marx, Lukàcs, Girard et la sociologie du roman," *Médiations*, 2 (1961). Basis for article cited in II-1963-A and I-1964-A-2.

61/3   "La democratie économique et la création culturelle," in RIS, 1-2 (1961), pp. 239-58.

62/1   "Problèmes d'une sociologie du roman," in *Cahiers internationaux de sociologie*, vol. XXXII (Jan.-June, 1962), pp. 61-72. (See V-61/2.)

62/1   *"Introduction aux premiers écrits de Georg Lukàcs,"   XIV-16 TM, 195 (Aug., 1962), pp. 254-80. Also appears as:
      a. "Les écrits de jeune Lukàcs," afterword to G. Lukàcs, *La Théorie du roman* (Paris: Gonthier, 1963).

62/3   "Marylin, ce negatif de notre temps," *France-Observateur*, 644 (Sept. 6, 1962), pp. 21-22.

62/4   "Structure de la tragedie racinienne," in Jean Lacquot, *Le Théâtre tragique: etudes de G. Antoine (e.a.) réunies et presentées par Jean Jacquot* (Paris: CNRS, 1962). Paper presented at the Colloque d'Anvers (June 19-22, 1959).

62/5   "La place d'*Andromaque* dans l'oeuvre de Racine," in CRB, 40 (Nov., 1962), pp. 107-119.

62/6   "Diderot, la pensée des 'lumières' et la dialectique," in *Médecine de France*, 136 (1962), pp. 33-40.

63/1   "Lumières et dialectique" (June, 1959), in *Utopies et Institutions au XVIIIe siècle: le pragmtisme des Lumières*, ed Pierre Francastel (Paris, The Hague: Mouton & Co., 1963), pp. 305-14.

64/1 "A propos de *'Le Mariage'* de Gombrowicz," in *France-Observateur*, 718 (Feb. 6, 1964).

64/2 "Préface" to Gérard Namer, *L'Abbe Lé Roy et ses amis. Essai sur le jansénisme extrémiste extra-mondain* (Paris: SEVPEN, 1964), pp. 7-8.

65/1 "Ces intellectuels sans attache. A propos de Karl Korsch: "Marxisme et philosophie," *Le nouvel observateur*, 17 (March 11, 1965).

65/2 *"To the Memory of Paul Alexander Baran," *Monthly Review*, Vol. 16 (March, 1965), p. 105.   XIV-17

65/3 "Le livre et la lecture dans les sociétés industrielles modernes," *Le Drapeau* (Montreal, Oct., 1965).

66/1 "Les rapports de la pensée de Georges Lukàcs avec l'oeuvre de Kierkegaard" (1964), in *Kierkegaard vivant*, colloquium organized by UNESCO (Paris, Apr. 21-23, 1964) (Paris: Gallimard, 1966), pp. 125-64. (See V-73/1.)

66/2 "Jean Piaget et la philosophie," in *Jean Piaget et les sciences sociales. A l'occasion de son 70e anniversaire, Cahiers Vilfredo Pareto*, 10 (Nov., 1966), pp. 5-23.

66/3 "Sur le probleme de l'objectivite en sciences sociales," in *Psychologie et epistémologie génétique. Themes piagetiens. Hommage à Jean Piaget avec une bibliographie de ses oeuvres* (Paris: Dunod, 1966).

67/1 "Pascal und Port-Royal" (1960), in *Weltflucht und Politik* (Berlin and Neuwied, Hermann Luchterhand Verlag, 1967). Contains the above article (not previously published) plus German translations of articles in RD (I-1959-A-II-1, 2 and 4).

67/2 *Pascal*, Italian trans. by Lisa Baruffi (Milan: Compagnia Edizioni Internazionali, 1967).

67/3 "Conditions de l'interprétation dialectique," in *L'Ambivalence dans la culture arabe* (Paris: Anthropos, 1967), pp. 356-58.

67/4 "Actualité de la pensée de Karl Marx" (1964), in HS, 4 (Apr.-June, 1967), pp. 37-47.

67/5 "Epistémologie de la sociologie" (1965), in *Logique et connaissance scientifique*, directed by Jean Piaget (Paris:

Gallimard, Encyclopedie de la Pleiade, 1967), pp. 992-1018.

68/1   "Les sciences humaines doivent-elles intégrer la philosophie?" in *Recherche et science de l'homme* (3e trim., 1968), pp. 9-32.

68/2   "Pourquoi les étudiants?" in HS, 8 (1968), pp. 3-24. First presentation (pp. 3-7) at a round table discussion (May 23, 1968), with Jacques Berque, Serge Jonas, Henri Lefebvre, etc.

68/3   "Débat sur l'autogestion," in *Autogestion. Etudes, débats, documents* (Cahier 7, December, 1968), pp. 57-61 and 64-71. The major comments of Goldmann and Serge Mallet made at a round table discussion of autogestion organized by *Le Nouvel observateur* (Paris, July 7, 1968).

68/4   "La denuncia sociologica e culturale" (1967), ed. Brigitte Navelet from a conference presentation by Goldmann, and trans. into Italian by Ernesto Rubin de Cervin, in *Participazione, denuncia, escorcismo nel teatro d'oggi* (Venice: La Biennale di Venezia, 1968).

69/1   "Premessa a 'La reificazione' " (written in Apr., 1969 as an introduction to "La réification" [RD: I-1959-A-I-4]), trans. Giusi Oddo, in *Ideologie*, 8 (Rome, 1969), pp. 122-25.

69/2   "Idéologie et marxisme" (July 19, 1967), in *Le Centenaire du "Capital." Exposés et entretiens sur le marxisme* (Paris, The Hague: Mouton & Co., 1969), pp. 297-334; followed by a discussion of the article, pp. 344-41. Paper presented at a colloquium on the 100th anniversary of *Capital* at Cérisy-La-Salle, July 11-20, 1967. Goldmann also participates in a discussion of a paper by Anouar Abdel-malek on "Marxisme et liberation nationale," pp. 285-88.

69/3   "La mort d'Adorno," in *La Quinzaine Littéraire*, 78 (Sept. 1-15, 1969), pp. 26-27.

69/4   "Préface" of Fernand Dumont, *La dialectique de l'objet économique* (Paris: Anthropos, 1969), pp. vii-xiv.

69/5   Présentation de l'exposition Antonio Bueno and Silvio Loffredo, catalogue of the exposition at Galerie G 30, *Eco d'arte*, 6 (June, 1969).

70/1   "Structure sociale et conscience des structures," in *Structuralisme et marxisme*, introduction by Victor Leduc (Paris: Union générale d'Editions, 1970). Goldmann's contribution to a discussion with Ernest Labrousse, Andre Martinet, Albert Soboul, Pierre Vidal-Naquet, etc., of Labrousse's "Structure sociale et histoire," presented at a colloquium organized by *Raison Présente* under Leduc's direction, and first published in *Raison Présente*, 7 (July-Sept., 1968), pp. 50-53. Other interventions by Goldmann at the colloquium appear in *Structuralisme et marxisme*, pp. 145-46, 156, 174-75, 193-94, 197-98, 200-04.

70/2   "Structuralisme génétique et analyse stylistique," in *Linguaggi nella società nella tecnica* (Milan: Edizioni di Comunità, 1970), pp. 143-61.

70/3   *"Structure: Human Reality and Methodological Concept" (Dec., 1966), in *The Structuralist Controversy: The Languages of Criticism and the Sciences of Man*, ed. R. Macksey and E. Donato (Baltimore: Johns Hopkins Press, 1970); followed by a discussion of the article with J. Hyppolite, J.-P. Vernant, R. Schneider, J. Lacan, etc. The French original is "Structure: realité humaine et concept méthodologique."

71/1   *"Eppur Si Muove" (Feb., 1969), English trans.   XIV-19
by Tom Wengraf, in *The Spokesman*, 15-16 (Aug.-Sept., 1971).

71/2   "Sujet et objet en sciences humaines" (1969), RP, 17 (Jan.-March, 1971), pp. 83-101.

71/3   *"Reflections on *History and Class Consciousness*"   XIV-20
English trans. by Peter France, in *Aspects of History and Class Consciousness*, ed. Istvan Mészáros (London: Routledge & Kegan Paul, 1971), pp. 65-84. The French original remains unpublished.

71/4   "Littérature (Sociologie de la)" (1970), in *Encyclopaedia Universalis*, vol. X (1971), pp. 7-10.

71/5   "Lukács, Gyorgy" (1970), in *Encyclopaedia Universalis*, vol. X (1971), pp. 138-40.

71/6   "Révolution et bureaucratie." Paper read at a colloquium at Cabris on "Sociologie et Révolution" (July, 1970), in HS, 21 (July-Sept., 1971).

73/1   "Choix de Textes," in LG, pp. 97-148. (See VIII-3.) Includes excerpts from SHP, DC, RD, MS; plus an excerpt, "Sur Lukács," from *Kierkegaard Vivant* (V-66/1), pp. 148-52; and an interview (see VII-70/2).

73/2   "A Propos des *Grundrisse*," "Remarques au sujet du chapitre sur l'argent" (Feb. 12, 1963), *"Les Grundrisse et Le Capital"* (Jan. 21, 1970), and "Sur le mode de production asiatique" (Apr. 15, 1970), in "Fragments inédits," LG, pp. 156-58. (See VIII-3-c.)

73/3   "Epistémologie differentielle et conscience possible: Projet de Recherche" (undated), in *ibid.*, pp. 159-62.

73/4   "Lukàcs et Heidegger," an excerpt from LH (I-1973-A), in RIS, 3/4 (1969), pp. 503-24 (see X-1973-B).

VI. GOLDMANN'S PARTICIPATION IN DISCUSSIONS (EXCLUDING THOSE INVOLVING HIS OWN PAPERS)

56/1   Discussion with J. Lacan, M. Merleau-Ponty, etc., about Claude Lévi-Strauss, "Sur les rapports entre la mythologie et le rituel" (Session of the Société française de Philosophie, May 26, 1956), published in BSFP, 3 (50e annee, July-Sept., 1956), pp. 123-24.

56/2   Discussion with J. Wahl, etc., about A.J. Ayer, "La mémoire" (Dec. 1, 1956), in BSFP, 4 (50e.année, Oct.-Dec., 1956), pp. 205-6.

57/1   Colloquium on *Descartes, Cahiers de Royaumont. Philosophie II* (Paris: Ed. de Minuit), pp. 55, 138-39, 257-59, 270-71, 477.

58/1   Discussion with F. Alquie, M. and E. Souriau, J. Wahl, etc., about Gabriel Marcel, "L'être devant la pensée interrogative" (Jan. 25, 1958), BSFP, 1 (52e année, Jan.-March, 1958), p. 26.

58/2   Discussion with H. Lefebvre, M. Souriau, J. Wahl, etc., about Georges Gurvitch, "Structures sociales et multiplicité des temps" (Jan. 31, 1959), BSFP, 3 (52e année, July-Dec., 1958), pp. 130-33.

60/1   Participation in *Atti del XII Congresso Internazionale di Filosofia* (1958), vol. II, *L'uomo e la natura* (Florence: G.C. Sansoni, 1960).

61/1   Interventions at the Recontre internationale de Royaumont (May 17-20, 1961), about J.-G. Gurvitch, "Le sort des structures sociales," and Charles de Lauwe, "L'expansion des besoins et l'evolution de l'humanité," in *Quel avenir attend l'homme?* (Paris: PUF, 1961), pp. 167-68, 247.

62/1   Colloquium on *La Philosophie analytique, Cahiers de Royaumont, Philosophie IV* (Paris: Ed. de Minuit, 1962).

63/1   Discussion of Georges Gusdorf, "Les sciences humaines et la philosophie" (Nov. 24, 1962), BSFP, 2 (57e année, July-Sept., 1963), pp. 92-95.

64/1   Discussion of "Littérature et stylistique—Les visages de la critique depuis 1920—Molière," at the 25th Congrès de l'Association Internationale des Etudes Françaises (Paris, College de France, July 25-27, 1963); published in *Cahiers de l'association internationale des études françaises*, 16 (March, 1964), pp. 289, 294.

65/1   Discussions with E. Bloch, J. Derrida, L. Kolakowski, S. Mallet and J. Piaget, etc., about their papers at the colloquium on genesis and structure (July-Aug., 1959—see I-1970/1-A-16); published in Gandillac, Goldmann *et al.*, ENGS.

67/1   Discussion about "Sociologie de la 'construction nationale,' dans les Nouveaux Etats," at the sixth colloquium of the Association Internationale des Sociologues de Langue française (Royaumont, Oct. 28-30, 1965), in RIS, 2-3 (1967), pp. 558-61.

68/1   Discussion of M.D. Chenu, "Orthodoxie et hérésie. Le point de vue du Théologien," and discussion with J. Orcibal and G. Le Bras about Chapters V and VI, part two of DC (pp. 97-156)—in a colloquium on "Hérésie et société au XVIIe siècle: le cas janséniste" (Royaumont, May 27-30, 1962); published in *Hérésies et société dans l'Europe preindustrielle—XIe-XVIIe siècles*, presented by Jacques Le Goff (Paris, The Hague: Mouton & Co., 1968).

68/2   Discussion of Jacques Derrida, "La 'Difference' " (presented Jan. 17, 1968), BSFP, 3 (62e annee, July-Sept., 1968), pp. 110-113.

69/1   Discussion of "Qu'est-ce qu'un auteur?" BSFP, 3 (63e année, July-Sept., 1969).

73/1   "Débat Goldmann—Lucien Sebag (Sur les Manuscripts de 1844)" (April, 1962), in "Fragments inédits," LG, pp. 151-2. (See VIII-3-c.)

73/2   "Débat Goldmann—Marcuse (1961-62)" (Dec. 5 and 9, 1961; Feb. 17, 1962), in *ibid.*, pp. 152-55.

73/3   *Discussion with T.W. Adorno, published as   XIII-7-c
        "Discussion extraite des actes du second colloque international sur la sociologie de la littérature tenue a Royaumont" (Jan., 1968), in *Hommage à Lucien Goldmann*, RIS, 3/4 (1973—see X-1973-B), pp. 525-42. Scheduled to appear in *Decrire, comprendre, expliquer* (Brussels: EISULB).

VII. INTERVIEWS

64/1 Interview with Victor Flores Olea, *Revista de la Universidad de Mexico* (April, 1964).

64/2 Interview with Lorenzo Batallan, *Caracas* (Nov. 1, 1964).

64/3 Interview with Guillermo and Julieta Sucre, *Zona Franca*, 5 (Caracas, 1re année, November, 1964).

66/1 "Structuralisme, marxisme, existentialisme," HS, 2 (Oct.-Dec., 1966), pp. 105-124. This consists of almost the entire interview with Iliga Bojovic for Belgrade Radio-Television:
   a. Serbo-Croatian trans. appeared in *Sociajalism*, 9 (Belgrade, Sept. 1966).
   b. Slav trans., "Dimenzije i smerovi filozofske misli," appeared in *Odjek*, 21 (Sarajevo, Nov. 1, 1966).

68/1 Interview on "L'Université," in *L'Express*, Supplement II (June 3, 1968).
   a. "Rectificatif à propos de l'article, 'L'Université'," in Supplement II, *L'Express*, 884 (June 17-23, 1968).

68/2 Interview by Michele Georges on "La croyance en Dieu," *L'Express*, 892 (Aug. 12, 1968).

68/3 Interview with Jacques Leenhardt on "Sociologia de la Literatura," in *Diario*, 206 (Madrid, May 8, 1968).

69/1 Interview by Michel Carael on "Le mouvement de Mai 1968 et les nouvelles possibilités de mise en cause globale de la société capitaliste avancée," in *Mai*, 6 (Brussels, June-July, 1969), pp. 38-40.

69/2 "Filozofski Angazman i Angazovanje Filozofa" [The commitment of philosophers and committed philosophy], interview by Jasmina Alic, in *Lica*, 20-22 (Sarajevo, July-Sept., 1969).

69/3 "La pluridisciplinarité," interview with Jean-Pierre Tadros, in *Le Devoir* (Montreal, Oct. 4, 1969).

70/1 "Arta si discipline umane," interview with Ion Pascadi, *Romania Literaria*, 25 (Bucharest, June 18, 1970).

70/2 "La théorie," interview with Brigitte Devisme, *VH 101*, 2 (Summer, 1970), pp. 35-45. Reprinted as "Bilan théorique," in "Choix de Textes," LG, pp. 134-48 (see VIII-3-b).

71/1   Interview on the problems of the Middle East (April, 1970), in *Israel-Palestine*, 3/4 (Brussels, 1971).

73/1   Interview with Marthe Robert (July 1, 1969), *Psychanalyse et Sociologie comme méthodes d'étude des phénomènes historiques et culturels*, Vol. II of *Critique sociologique et critique psychanalytique* (Brussels: ESL, EISULB, 1973), pp. 77-84. (See II-1970-A.)

VIII. BOOKS ON GOLDMANN (See also XV-15)

1. Franco Crispini, *Lo strutturalismo dialettico di Lucien Goldmann* (Naples: Libreria Scientifica, 1970). Collection "Quaderni di Filosofia," vol. XI. Istituto di Storia della Filosofia dell'Università di Napoli. Includes:
   a. Bibliography (see XI).   XIII-7-d

2. Rudolf Heyndels, *Cohérence ésthetique et insertion sociale* (*Réflexion sur la pensée de Lucien Goldmann*). Memoire dactylographie dépose a l'Université Libre de Bruxelles (1972-73). Stagaire de recherches au FNRS. For separately published excerpts, see

3. Sami Nair and Michael Lowy, *Lucien Goldmann ou la dialectique de la totalité* (Paris: Editions Seghers, 1973). Contains:
   a. Introductory Study, pp. 8-95.
   b. "Choix de Textes," pp. 97-148 (see V-73/1 and VII-70/2).
   c. "Fragments inédits," taken from Lowy's notes on Goldmann's classroom sessions at the Ecole Pratique des Hautes Etudes, pp. 151-62 (see V-73/2 and 3, and VI-73/1 and 2).
   d. "Bibliographie," by Brigitte Navelet, pp. 163-69.   XIII-7-d

4. Pierre V. Zima, *Goldmann, dialectique de l'immanence* (Paris: Editions Universitaires). In addition to the text itself, it contains:
   a. Annie Goldmann, "Biographie de Lucien Goldmann," pp. 125-27; reprinted from SC (I-1971/1-A).
   b. "Bibliographie" by Brigitte Navelet, pp. 128-34.   XIII-7-d

IX. BOOKS DRAWING ON OR INSPIRED BY GOLDMANN
    (See also XVI-A.)

1. Charles Castella, *Structures romanesques et vision sociale chez Maupassant*. Preface by Rene Girard (Paris: Ed. de l'Age d'Homme, 1972).

2. Juan Ignacio Ferreras, *Teoria y Práxis de la Novela. La ultima aventura de Don Quijote* (Paris: Ediciones Hispoamericanas, 1970).

3. ————, *La Novela de Ciencia Ficcion. Interpretacion de una novela marginal* (Madrid: Siglo XXI de España Editores, 1972).

4. Annie Goldmann, *Cinéma et société moderne. Le cinéma de 1958 à 1968: Godard—Antonioni—Resnais—Robbe-Grillet* (Paris: Anthropos, 1971).

5. Jacques Leenhardt, *Lecture politique du roman: La Jalousie d'Alain Robbe-Grillet* (Paris: Editions de Minuit, 1972).

6. Michael Lowy, *La théorie de la révolution chez le jeune Marx* (Paris: Maspero, 1970).

7. Geneviève Mouillaud, *Le Rouge et le Noir de Stendhal, le roman possible* (Paris: Larousse, 1972).

8. Narcisco Pizarro, *Analysis estructural de la Novela* (Madrid: Siglo XXI de España Editores, 1973)—especially chapter 3.

X. COLLECTIONS OF ARTICLES ON GOLDMANN OR APPLYING HIS METHOD

1969   A. *Sociologie de la littérature. Recherches récentes et discussions.* RIS, 3 (ESL III, 1969). Edited and containing several articles by Goldmann (see II-1969-A and A-1), this collection also contains "Goldmannian" articles by students and associates.
  1. Willy Delsipech, " 'Les Chats': essai d'analyse formelle," pp. 415-26.
  2. Jacques Leenhardt, "Semantique et sociologie de la littérature," pp. 427-40.
  3. Nicolas Bonhote, "Aperçus sur une analyse sociologique de l'oeuvre de Marivaux," pp. 441-48.
  4. Bernard Laudy, "La vision tragique de Madame de La Fayette, ou une jansénisme athée," pp. 449-62.
  5. Annie Goldmann, "Les deserts de la foi," pp. 463-74.
  6. George Huaco, "Sociologie du roman: Le roman mexicain, 1915-1965," pp. 479-84.
  7. Jack Warwick, "Un cas type d'application de la méthode sociologique: Les écrivains canadiens-français et leur situation minoritaire," pp. 485-502.
  8. Michel Brule, "Introduction à l'Univers de Marie-Claire Blais," pp. 503-14.
  9. J. Elsberg, "La sociologie dans l'étude bourgeoise contemporaine de la littérature," pp. 525-38.

1973   B. *Hommage à Lucien Goldmann.* RIS 3/4 (1973). Including materials by Goldmann (see V-73/4 and VI-73/3), this volume is mainly a collection of articles about him and his theory:

      1. R. Lallemand, "En guise d'introduction," pp. 499-503.

    *2. H. Marcuse, "Some General Remarks on   XIII-7-b Lucien Goldmann," pp. 543-44.

    *3. J. Piaget, "Bref temoinage," pp. 545-48.   XIII-7-a

      4. J. Duvignaud, "Goldmann et la vision du monde," pp. 549-55.

      5. J. Leenhardt, "A propos de *Marxisme et sciences humaines*," pp. 555-63.

      6. G. Lukàcs, "Remarques sur la théorie de l'Histoire littéraire," pp. 563-96.

      7. E. Kohler, "Le hasard littéraire, le possible et la necessité," pp. 597-612.

      8. A. Goldmann, "*Salamnbo* ou l'Histoire absente," pp. 613-24.

      9. A. Krutwig Caers et le Groupe de travail du Centre de Sociologie de la Littérature (Brussels), "La vision du monde dans le 'Pétits Poèms en prose' de Ch. Baudelaire," pp. 625-40.

    10. G. Mouillaud, " 'Roman' (article pour le dictionnaire de la sociologie de la littérature en preparation sous la direction de L. Goldmann)," pp. 641-50.

    11. L. and N. Rudich, "Eugenie Grandet, martyr du capitalisme," pp. 651-70.

    12. Y. Ishaghpour, "Citizen Kane et les antinomies de la pensée bourgeoise," pp. 671-712.

    13. Fr. Gaillard, "*Le roi est mort.* Note sur la vision du monde dans un drame de E. Ionesco," pp. 713-31.

    14. E. Esaer, "G. Lukàcs—L. Goldmann: l'Aventure discursive," pp. 732-86.

    *15. E. Tell, "Bibliographie de Lucien Goldmann,"   XIII-7-d pp. 787-806.

XI. WORKS CONTAINING COMMENTARIES ON GOLDMANN[1]

1. A.A.V.V., *Les chémins actuels de la critique* (Paris, 1968).

2. R.-M. Albérès, "Sur le méta-roman," *Les Nouvelles Littéraires* (Dec. 19, 1963), p. 5.

3. Ferdinand Alquié, "Pascal et la critique contemporaine," *Critique* (Nov., 1975), pp. 953-67.

*4. Roland Barthes, *Sur Racine* (Paris: Ed. du Seuil, 1963)   XVI-A-1

---

1. Based on listings by Franco Crispini (see VIII-1-a) and Laurent Le Sage (see XV-4). Crispini (p. 114) points to a valuable checklist of early Goldmann criticism, which we have been unable to find: "Extrait de la *Revue de l'Institut de sociologie de Bruxelles,* 3/69, pp. 211-229."

5. Maurice Blanchot, "L'Homme au point zero," *Nouvelle revue française*, new series, Vol. VI (April, 1956).
6. C. Bouazis, *Littérarité et société* (Paris, 1971).
7. R. Boudon, *Les méthodes en sociologie* (Paris: PUF, 1970).
8. Pierre Daix, *Nouvelle critique et art moderne* (Paris: Le Seuil, 1968).
*9. Serge Doubrovsky, *Pourquoi la nouvelle critique?*   XVI-A-2
Critique et objectivite (Paris: Mercure de France, 1966).
10. J. Elsberg, "La sociologie dans l'étude bourgeoise contemporaine de la littérature," extract from *Voprosy Literatury*, 41 (1967).
11. Rene Girard, "Racine, pète de la gloire," *Critique* (June, 1964), pp. 483-506.
12. M. Robert Emmet Jones, *Panorama de la nouvelle critique en France. De Gaston Bachelard à J.-P. Weber* (Paris: SEDES, 1968).
*13. Raymond Picard, *Nouvelle critique ou nouvelle*   XVI-A-3
imposture? (Paris: Pauvert, 1965).
14. G. Scalla, *Critica, Lettera, Ideologia* (Rome: Marsilio Editori, 1968).

XII. RECENT EUROPEAN ARTICLES ON GOLDMANN

1. E. Esaer, "G. Lukàcs—L. Goldmann. L'Aventure discursive. Lecture Semantique d'un discourse neo-hegelian matérialista (II)," RIS, 1 (1974). See X-B-14 for Part I of this essay.
2. Rudolf Heyndels, "Réflexion sur la notion de 'cohérence' dans la théorie de Lucien Goldmann," in RIS, 3/4 (1974), pp. 3-23. See VIII-2.
3. ————, "Vision du monde et réification—Réflexion sur la sociologie de la littérature de Lucien Goldmann," RIS, 1/2 (1974), pp. 593-619. See VIII-2.
4. Jean-Michel Palmier, "Goldmann Vivant," *Praxis*, 3/4 (1971), pp. 567-624.
5. Rodolphe Roelens, "Les avatars de la médiation dans la sociologie de Lucien Goldmann," HS, 15 (Jan.-March, 1970), pp. 295-316.

XIII. BOOKS BY GOLDMANN IN ENGLISH

1. *Immanuel Kant*, trans. Robert Black (London: I-1947-C
New Left Books, 1971).
2. *The Human Sciences and Philosophy*, trans.   I-1952-B
Hayden V. White and Robert Anchor (London: Jonathan Cape, 1964).
3. *The Hidden God: A Study of Tragic Vision in the*   I-1955-A
Pensées of Pascal and the Tragedies of Racine, trans. Philip Thody (London: Routledge and Kegan Paul; New York: Humanities Press, 1964).
4. *Racine*, trans. Alastair Hamilton and introduction by   I-1956-A
Raymond Williams (slightly revised version of XV-13) (Cambridge: Rivers Press Ltd., 1969).
5. *Towards a Sociology of the Novel*, trans. Alan Sheridan. I-1964-B

(London: Tavistock, 1975).

6. *The Philosophy of the Enlightenment: The Burgess*   I-1970-1-A-2
and the Enlightenment, trans. Henry Maas (London: Routledge and Kegan Paul; Cambridge, Mass.: MIT Press, 1973).

7. *Cultural Creation in Modern Society*, trans.   I-1971/2
by Bart Grahl, introduction by William Mayrl, appendices trans. and compiled by Ileana Rodriguez and Marc Zimmerman (St. Louis: Telos Press, 1976). Appendices include:

  a. J. Piaget, "A Brief Tribute to Lucien Goldmann"   X-1973-B-3

  b. H. Marcuse, "Some General Remarks on   X-1973-B-2
Lucien Goldmann"

  c. T.W. Adorno and L. Goldmann, "To Describe,   VI-73/3
Understand and Explain."

  d. "Lucien Goldmann: A Bibliography." Based on X-1973-B-15, VIII-1-a and VIII-3-d and 4-b; see also XV-4 for XI.

XIV. ENGLISH TRANSLATIONS OF ARTICLES BY GOLDMANN

1. "Ideology and Writing," *The Times Literary Supplement*   I-1952-C-1
(London, Sept. 28, 1967), pp. 903-905.

2. "The Moral Universe of the Playwright," from *The*   I-1955-A
Hidden God (i-3), in Elizabeth and Tom Burns, eds., *Sociology of Literature and Drama* (Harmondsworth, Middlesex, England: Penguin Books, 1973), pp. 311-318.

3. "Dialectical Materialism and Literary History,"   I-1959-A-3
in *New Left Review*, 92 (July-Aug., 1975), pp. 39-51.

4. "Is There a Marxist Sociology?" in *International*   I-1959-A-III-3
Socialist, 34.

5. "Introduction to the Problems of a Sociology of   I-1964-A-2
the Novel," trans. by Beth Blumenthal, *Telos*, 18 (Winter, 1973-74), pp. 122-35.

6. "Genetic-Structuralist Method in History of Literature,"   I-1964-A-5
trans. by Forrest Williams, in *Marxism and Art: Writings in Aesthetics and Criticism*, ed. Berel Lang and Forrest Williams (New York: David McKay Co., 1972), pp. 243-55. Also published as:

  a. "Genetic Structuralism and the History of Literature," trans. by Catherine and Richard Macksey, in *Velocities of Change: Critical Essays from Modern Language Notes*, ed. Richard A. Macksey (Baltimore: Johns Hopkins Univ. Press, 1974), pp. 89-104.

7. "The Theatre of Sartre," trans. by Sandy MacDonald,   I-1970/1-A-7
in *The Drama Review*, 15 (Fall, 1970-T-49), pp. 102-119.

8. "The Theater of Gombrowicz," trans. Patricia   I-1970/1-A-8
Dreyfus, in TDR, 14 (Spring, 1970-T-47), pp. 102-112.

9. "The Theatre of Jean Genet; A Sociological   I-1970/1-A-10-a
Study," trans. Patricia Dreyfus, ed. Richard Schechner, in TDR, 12

(Winter, 1968-T-38). Condensed version of article in CRB, 57; also appears in:
  a. *The Theatre of Jean Genet: A Casebook*, ed. Richard N. Coe (New York: Grove Press, 1970), pp. 220-38.

10. "Criticism and Dogmatism in Literature," trans.   I-1970/2-A-3
    by Ilona Halberstadt, in *To Free a Generation: The Dialectics of Liberation*, ed. David Cooper (Macmillan, 1969), pp. 128-149.

11. "The Sociology of Literature: Status and Problems   I-1970/2-A-4
    of Method," *International Social Sciences Journal*, XIX, 4 (1967), pp. 493-516. Also appears in:
    a. *The Sociology of Art and Literature: A Reader*, ed. Milton C. Albrecht, James Barnett and Mason Griff (New York: Praeger Publishers, 1970), pp. 582-610.

12. "*The German Ideology* and the 'Theses on   I-1970/2-A-8
    Feuerbach'," introduction to Karl Marx and Friedrich Engels, *The German Ideology* (London: Penguin Books, 1970).

13. "The Aesthetics of the Young Lukács," in *New*   I-1970/2-A-11
    Hungarian Quarterly, 47 (Vol. XIII, Autumn, 1972), pp. 129-35.

14. "Socialism and Humanism," trans. Edouard   I-1970/2-A-14
    Roditi, in *Socialist Humanism: An International Symposium*, ed. Erich Fromm (Garden City, New York: Doubleday and Co., 1965), pp. 38-49. Also published in London: Allen Lane, 1967.

15. "Genetic Structuralism in the Sociology of Literature,"   II-1967-A-1
    trans. Petra Morrison, in *Sociology of Literature and Drama*, ed. Elizabeth and Tom Burns (Harmondsworth, Middlesex, England: Penguin Books, 1973), pp. 109-23.

16. "The Early Writings of Georg Lukács," trans. by   V-62/2
    Joy N. Humes, in *Triquarterly*, 9 (1967), pp. 165-81.

17. "To the Memory of Paul Alexander Baran," *Monthly*   V-65/2
    Review, 16:11 (New York, March, 1965), p. 105.

18. "Structure: Human Reality and Methodological   V-70/3
    Concept" (Dec., 1966), in *The Structuralist Controversy: The Languages of Criticism and the Sciences of Man*, ed. Robert Macksey and Eugenio Donato (Baltimore: Johns Hopkins Univ. Press, 1970), pp. 98-110. An article, followed by a discussion with J. Hyppolite, J.-P. Vernant, R. Schechner, J. Lacan, etc.

19. "Eppur Si Muove" (Feb., 1969), trans. by Tom Wengraf,   V-71/1
    in *The Spokesman*, 15-16 (Aug.-Sept., 1971).

20. "Reflections on *History and Class Consciousness*"   V-71/3
    (Jan., 1970), trans. by Peter France, in *Aspects of History and Class Consciousness*, ed. István Mészáros (London: Routledge and Kegan Paul, 1971), pp. 65-84.

21. "Understanding Marcuse," in *Partisan*   I-1970/2-A-13
    Review, 3 (1971), pp. 247-62.

XV. WORKS IN ENGLISH DEVOTED TO GOLDMANN

1. William Boelhower, "Lucien Goldmann, Towards a Sociology of the Novel," *The Minnesota Review*, 6 (Spring, 1976), pp. 140-143.

2. Patrick Brady, "Socio-Criticism as Genetic Structuralism: Value and Limitations of the Goldmann Method," in *L'Esprit Createur*, 14:3, pp. 207-18.

3. Christine Glucksmann, "Lucien Goldmann: Humanist or Marxist?" in *New Left Review*, 56 (1969), pp. 49-62.

4. George Huaco, "Ideology and Literature," *New Literary History*, 3 (Spring, 1973), pp. 421-36.

5. Laurent Le Sage, "Lucien Goldmann," in *The French*　　　XIII-7-d *New Criticism* (Pennsylvania State Univ. Press, 1967), pp. 87-93.

6. Alastair McIntyre, "Pascal and Marx: On Lucien Goldmann's *Hidden God*," *Encounter* (Oct., 1964), pp. 69-76; reprinted in McIntyre's *Against the Self-Image of the Age* (London: Duckworth, 1971).

7. William Mayrl, "Introduction" to Lucien Goldmann, *Cultural Creation in Modern Society*, trans. by Bart Grahl (St. Louis: Telos Press, 1976), pp. 1-27. (See XII-7.)

8. William Mayrl, review of Lucien Goldmann, *The Philosophy of the Enlightenment*, *Telos*, 27 (Spring, 1976), pp. 199-208.

9. Francis Mulhern, "Introduction to Goldmann," *New Left Review*, 92 (July-Aug., 1975), pp. 34-38.

10. Scott Sanders, "Towards a Social Theory of Literature," *Telos*, 18 (Winter, 1973-74), pp. 107-121.

11. Robert Sayre, "Lucien Goldmann and the Sociology of Literature," *Praxis: A Journal of Radical Perspectives on the Arts*, 2 (Spring, 1976).

12. George Steiner, "Marxism and the Literary Critic" (1958), in Steiner's *Language and Silence: Essays on Language, Literature and the Inhuman* (New York: Atheneum, 1970), pp. 305-24.

13. Robert Weimann, "French Structuralism and Literary History: Some Critiques and Reconsiderations," trans. by Jack Zipes, in *New Literary History*, IV:3 (Spring, 1973), pp. 437-70.

14. Raymond Williams, "From Leavis to Goldmann: In Memory of Lucien Goldmann," *New Left Review*, 67 (June, 1971), pp. 3-18.
a. A slightly modified version appears as the Introduction to *Racine* (XIII-4).

15. Marc Zimmerman, *Genetic Structuralism: Lucien Goldmann's Answer to the Advent of Structuralism* (unpublished dissertation, University of California at San Diego, 1975). A revised version embodying XVI-C-3, is planned for publication by Indiana University Press, 1977; a Spanish translation is planned for publication by Editorial Tiempo Contemporaneo, Buenos Aires, 1977.

XVI. OTHER WORKS IN ENGLISH WITH COMMENTARIES ON GOLDMANN

A. Translations (See XI)

1. Roland Barthes, "History or Literature?" in *On*   XI-4
   Racine, trans. Richard Howard (New York: Hill and Wang, 1964),
   pp. 153-72.
2. Serge Doubrovsky, *The New Criticism in France*, trans. by   XI-9
   Derek Coltman (Chicago: Univ. of Chicago Press, 1973).
3. Raymond Picard, *New Criticism or New Fraud?*, trans by   XI-13
   Frank Towne (Pullman, Washington: Washington State Univ. Press,
   1969).

B. English-Language Originals

1. Jeremy Hawthorn, *Identity and Relationship: A Contribution to Marxist
   Theory of Literature* (London: Lawrence and Wishart, 1973).
2. Diana Laurenson and Alan Swingewood, *The Sociology of Literature*
   (London: MacGibbon and Kee, 1972), especially pp. 59-77.
3. Alan Swingewood, *The Novel and Revolution* (London: Macmillan,
   1976).

C. Unpublished Papers of Interest

1. Jonathan Bothelo, "Goldmann and La Rochefoucauld," paper presented
   at the French Section of the Marxist Literary Group, Modern Language
   Association (San Francisco, December 27, 1975).
2. Robert F. Kelly, "Social Action and Structural Theories: Considerations
   on Methodologies for the Sociology of Art," abbreviated version of "Historical Perspectives and Political Interpretations of Social Action Theory
   in the Sociology of Art," presented at the Pennsylvania Sociological
   Society meeting (Pennsylvania State University, November 1, 1975).
3. Ileana Rodriguez and Marc Zimmerman, "Lucien Goldmann and the
   Praxis in *Cultural Creation*," supplement to Zimmerman's *Genetic
   Structuralism* (XV-15), presented to the Minnesota Marxist Scholars
   (Minneapolis, January, 1976), and forthcoming in 1976 in *Telos*.